Walking the Wall

Life Behind Del Mar's "Snakewall"

Brier Miller Minor

Dayton Publishing

Dayton Publishing LLC
Solana Beach, CA 92075
publisher@daytonpublishing.com
www.daytonpublishing.com

ISBN: 978-1732526594

Printed in U. S. A.

Publisher's Cataloging-In-Publication Data
(Prepared by The Donohue Group, Inc.)

Names: Minor, Brier Miller, author.
Title: Walking the wall : life behind Del Mar's "Snakewall" / Brier Miller Minor.
Description: Solana Beach, CA : Dayton Publishing LLC, [2021] | Includes bibliographical references and index. | **Summary:** "This is the story of Del Mar's iconic 23-acre walled estate, La Atalaya, which was built by cement mogul Coy Burnett in the Roaring Twenties; struggled through the Great Depression, a devastating fire and World War II; and was lost to the Burnett family in 1971. The narrative also addresses the later decline and restoration of the property, and the effect of wealth, and its loss, on family dynamics." —Provided by publisher.
Identifiers: ISBN 9781735171609 (hardcover) | ISBN 9781732526594 (paperback)
Subjects: LCSH: Del Mar (Calif.)--Buildings, structures, etc.--History. | Dwellings--California--Del Mar--History. | Burnett family. | Rich people--California--Del Mar--History.
Classification: LCC F869.D45 M56 2021 | DDC 979.498--dc23

For my mother, Valentine,
and for Jessie,
who mothered us both

Viewed from the San Dieguito River Valley to the east, with new buildings on top of the ridge barely visible, La Atalaya looks much today as she did almost a century ago.

Contents

THE BURNETT FAMILY

Coy Burnett 1888–1971
Mildred Kingsbury Burnett 1887–1974

THEIR CHILDREN

Kingsbury Burnett (Gooding) 1916–2008
Her children: Neal and Owen

Anne Burnett (Craig) 1920–2010
Her children: John, Dana, Durrie and Karen

Coy Burnett, Junior 1925–1946

Valentine Burnett 1929–1994
August, 1948 married: Lloyd Winton Rentsch 1924–1970
Their children: Brier, Tim, Claire and Patrick

IN A CATEGORY ALL HER OWN

Jessie Wells Carter 1901–1973

OWNERS OF THE LOOKOUT / LA ATALAYA

before 1924: **Caroline Keller Schafer**

1924–1970s: **Coy and Mildred Burnett**

1977–mid 1990s: **James E. Smith**

1995–present: **Ron and Lucille Neeley**

Introduction

Walking the Wall

I want to tell you a story. It's my story, at least in part, but it doesn't belong to me. It's a story of place, and like many places, this one has witnessed generations of communities and families, holding firm while all sorts of stories played out through the years. And the place lives on, beckoning, quietly guarding the history, the memories, always offering the opportunity for new tales to develop.

My sister and brothers and I have each found reasons to return there, pilgrimages back to sunny memories of the freedom and adventures only children seem to have. Now I record them, for you, for those who are as fond of Del Mar, California as I am, and for others remembering stories of their own place.

Let me introduce you to my grandparents, who, in the Roaring Twenties, purchased an Arts and Crafts–style house atop the highest hill in the lovely seaside village of Del Mar. My grandfather's newly made wealth as a "cement mogul" in the boom town of Los Angeles allowed them to buy the vacation home, with its 360-degree view over the vast sparkling Pacific Ocean to the west, and to the north and east the San

A 1912 view to the west from the property where La Atalaya would be built a little more than a decade later

Dieguito River and its wide valley. In addition to the house, they bought 22 adjacent hilly acres covered in eucalyptus, acacias and rare Torrey pines, the makings of a unique estate. They named their property "La Atalaya" (*lah-ah-tah-LYE-ah*), Spanish for The Lookout, honoring the view. And she flourished and fell and picked herself back up and lives on today, as splendid as ever.

La Atalaya, this exquisite place by the sea, doesn't belong to my family anymore. But as the San Dieguito and La Jollan people knew when they lived here thousands of years ago, places don't ever really belong to us. If we're lucky, though, we belong to them.

A photo taken from La Atalaya in the 1930s showing the view to the northeast over the San Dieguito River Valley

Prologue, 1994

"Now I'll never know if OJ did it."

My mother, Valentine, was lying in her bed in a nursing home near Brentwood, California, a grim, thankfully brief, stay. She wasn't doing well. Earlier that day my husband, Bruce, had taken our kids to San Diego to look at colleges, and I had stayed behind to keep my mother company.

With only one lung left, Mama was having trouble breathing, which made it hard to talk. So we decided to watch TV, as we had done so often these past months, favoring movies, preferably old classics.

It was the middle of June and the Southern California sun spilled through the large window in her room. The warm golden sunlight and the bright blue lobelia in its hanging pot were just beyond the glass, yet an impossible distance from the cold metal bed that held my mother.

Sticking slightly to the olive green pleather armchair where I sat next to her bed, I clicked through the channels on the boxy television hanging on the wall opposite, looking for vintage Hepburn (preferably Audrey), Garland or Astaire. But every station seemed to be playing the same show: a white Ford Bronco slow-racing down the freeway followed by police cars, their sirens blaring. A banner appeared at the bottom of the screen:

BREAKING NEWS !!

Curious, we watched, and soon found our eyes glued to the TV. After all, how often do you get to see a real-life car chase?

Later that afternoon Bruce and the kids showed up, with stories of the campuses they had visited. But they were most excited to tell us about the strange sight, coming back on the freeway, of every lane in the opposite direction being completely empty except for a lone white truck being pursued by a whole bunch of cops.

We filled them in, all of us agog with the news of grisly murders only blocks away from the nursing home where my mother lay, not to mention the arrest of a famous football player named OJ, who had tried to escape. All the excitement seemed to distract my mother from Bruce's other news.

Returning from the college tours, he had taken a little detour and driven by La Atalaya, my grandparents' old property in Del Mar. Knowing how central it was to my childhood, he wanted to show the kids.

"It sure wasn't what I expected," he said. "There were signs posted." Not wanting to distress Mama, Bruce turned as he described the signs touting the "unique opportunity" for one's own mini-mansion on the grounds of the old estate.

"The property is being developed, broken up. They're advertising it as the largest walled estate on the West Coast or something." He said a couple of homes had already been built, their driveways slicing through the thick concrete wall my grandfather had erected so many years ago, encircling the entire 23-plus-acre property.

This was very sad news. It didn't matter that my family hadn't owned the estate for many years now, or that the cutting gardens and groves of avocado and citrus trees of my mother's youth were gone long before we had to sell it. La Atalaya and Del Mar were part of our family DNA, inseparable from our identity, and the thought of its being broken up seemed heartbreaking.

Standing beside Mama's bed I glanced over at her, worried about the impact of this news. Was she following our talk about the latest development in the saga of La Atalaya, her childhood home? She was groggy from medication, struggling to take precious oxygen into her remaining lung. I couldn't tell if she even heard.

She looked back at the television, drawn to the real-life car chase and the double-murder mystery.

It had been only ten months before that my 64-year-old mother, who had seemed perfectly fine, called me with the news that they'd found a tumor in her lung, and it was malignant.

"Does that mean you have lung cancer?"

"I don't know. They didn't say."

That was just the beginning of the half-understood descriptions and endless procedures that come to define the reality of a person with life-threatening illness. The new medical jargon became old hat as we progressed, learning to say things like "non–small cell cancer."

My mother and I walked much of this long 10-month journey together, through the "procedure" of a partial pneumonectomy that turned into removal of a whole lung, followed by the healing from an incision in the shape of a "J" that ran down the entire length of her spine, through the chemotherapy with its accompanying nausea and fatigue.

The final step, radiation, left her pale white chest scarlet and tender, like our noses when we were kids spending long days at the beach in Del Mar, the burned skin blistering, scabbing, layers peeling off to reveal the raw new skin beneath. Sometimes we'd rub zinc oxide on our noses, pure white against our rosy sunburns. Mama grew up going to that beach too, and her nose got just as burned.

But the radiation and all that treatment could not outfox the cancer. It had metastasized, and she had ended up in the nursing home, but not for long. It was just a week after the exciting real-life murder mystery when my mother was discharged from the nursing home and readmitted to the hospital. Clearly this would be her last admission.

The hospital, in Santa Monica, was being remodeled. Her room had previously been part of the pediatric unit. The remodel was not yet complete, and the walls were still decorated in happy reds and yellows, Mickey and Minnie Mouse at the beach wearing 1940s-era bathing suits and big smiles, carrying cute little pails and shovels. The cheerful colors seemed an incongruent, almost cruel, contrast to my mother's pallor, as she struggled to draw precious breath.

But Mama was a Southern California native and an avid moviegoer. The mother of four children in the 1950s and '60s, she'd seen her share of Disney. Maybe the cartoon characters were cheering her up. Maybe that explained why she looked at me with her wry smile, and started making jokes about dying and missing the denouement of a real-life whodunnit featuring a famous football player.

"Now I'll never know if OJ did it!"

I giggled. It felt good. "You'll probably find out before any of us do."

I was delighted when she laughed too. Though it seems a bit macabre now, I was grateful for the distraction the OJ drama provided my mother during her final days, the intrigue and suspense rivaling any fiction.

It was hard to believe we were close to the end of her life. She seemed almost lighthearted, cracking little jokes, apparently so relaxed that she decided to have a cocktail. She turned to Bruce and asked him to go out and get her a little bottle of Canadian Club, "like the ones on airplanes," and some club soda.

"Mama, do you really think you should be drinking?" I fussed like the overprotective parent of a daredevil child.

With a familiar lift of her eyebrows, my mother looked pointedly at the IV in her arm, supplying her with the maximum legal flow of morphine, the dosage her oncologist had assured her would keep the pain away even as it hastened her death. Then she looked up at me.

"Brier, what do you think will happen?"

We all laughed at that, and she did get her CC and soda. Watching her sip it, I was struck by how familiar, how normal it all seemed, my mother having a drink before dinner. And how impossible it was to imagine her gone, with her wide knowledge, her clever conversation, and her unusual history. How could an entire lifetime of travel and adventure and luxury and loss just evaporate into nothingness?

While she sipped her cocktail, we rehashed the latest conjecture about the glove that incriminated OJ but might or might not have been planted by the police. Then my mother grew reflective, and looked at me.

"You'd better ask me anything you want to know. Any questions at all…" she said.

I tried to think, but my brain was frozen. Finally, I came up with something.

"How come you never remarried?" Our father's death, a week before Christmas in 1970, had left her a 41-year-old widow, young, attractive, bright, lost.

"I never could figure out how to date," she said now. And then her smile asked the question, anything else?

I had only one thought: *This isn't happening!* Looking into her tired eyes, with their distinctive shade of blue gray violet – French blue, one of her favorite colors – I felt grateful for the easy intimacy that had slowly developed between us after my father's death. All I knew was that I wanted her to be at peace. So I smiled back and asked if she wanted to watch a movie.

And I didn't ask Valentine to talk about her family's beautiful estate in Del Mar, with its ornamental wall and gardens, the berry bushes and fruit trees, the stables, the chicken coops, the orchid house, the skeet shooting arena, the stands of Torrey pines. The enormous cistern, which we called "the reservoir."

I didn't inquire about her days growing up there along with her brother Coy Jr., and Jessie, her Black nanny, or ask her to describe one more time what it was like, being tutored at home by their mother's sister Maud, whom they called Aunty Too, while her older sisters lived at boarding school and their parents lived in a hotel in Los Angeles, 100 miles away.

I didn't want to remind her that the wall might soon come down.

Valentine Burnett Rentsch died on June 26, 1994, four months after her 65th birthday. Her pending death had prompted some ironic commentary about how many hours she'd put into deciding which Medicare supplemental insurance would be best. "Well, at least I got a few months' coverage out of all that research." That was my mother's way of dealing with it.

Always best to be witty, if given the choice, and facing death had stripped Mama of so many choices. Her death, like that of so many we lose, came way too early. As her doctor told her, "You're a very healthy woman – except for the cancer." Since her death I have had many opportunities to wish she could come back, if only to talk once more. One more chance to ask questions about the past or to fill her in on the OJ trial.

I'd love to tell her the wall is still there, thanks to the Del Mar City Council stepping in at the last moment, as in a good drama, to rescue the pristine property from the greedy developer.

She and I could swap stories, hers of long-ago Del Mar with its Tudor-style Stratford Inn, and mine about the man I thought was a gangster, who nearly destroyed La Atalaya. Or the surfer who would one day write in his blog about growing marijuana inside the wall (and she'd ask "What's a 'blog'?"). We'd have fun remembering the Warm Water Plunge, the big enclosed public pool in Del Mar, its salt water stinging our eyes in a different way than chlorine. It would be fun to reminisce about our childhoods, which, though a generation apart, held many memories in common – of the beach and our family home called La Atalaya, and, of course, of walking the wall.

I know my mother would love to hear what's happened to La Atalaya. I think she'd be pleased.

My grandparents' estate was born of fortune in a golden era. It held steady during the Depression, played a heroic role in World War II, survived a devastating fire, morphed into a funky vacation place, was lost to our family, teetered on the brink of destruction, fell into ruin and finally, rescued from under mountains of debris and trash, rose proudly from the ashes, a monument to wealth and light and sea.

How To Walk a Wall

The first, and arguably most critical, step in walking the wall that surrounded the entire estate at La Atalaya was to get on top of it. Most sections of the wall rose more than six feet from the ground, impossible for us kids to ascend, without a ladder at least. Fortunately, in one part of the property where we spent idyllic Augusts, the slope fell away so steeply that the wall had been set into the hill. While on the outside it was very high, inside the property it stood only about four feet above the ground. With a bit of a scramble, and not infrequent skinned knees or elbows, we were up on top, ready for adventure.

The concrete in the wall was not smooth. Rather than the evenness of a plastered interior wall, imagine running your hand along a rough, almost gravelly concrete surface. Perfect for scraping off layers of skin if we weren't careful, but better for holding on as we walked along the top. We may have worn sneakers sometimes, but in my memories, walking the wall was conducted while barefoot. At the beginning of each August our feet were a little tender, but after a week or so they had toughened up, from racing across the big expanse of concrete driveway in

At the spot where the wall was dug into the hill, there was only a four-foot vertical span between the ground and the top on the uphill side, inside the walled area. So we could scramble up.

front of the house and playing in the coarse sand in the side yard. Bare feet gave more grip, essential to staying on top of the wall, especially as it rose and fell steeply with the hills.

That was the trickiest part, the inclines. We always started by heading *up* the hill, gripping the wall with our hands and feet as we climbed along in a modified crawl, probably looking a bit like monkeys. As challenging as going up could be, it was a lot easier than the downward slope, which we left for later. As we got past the steepest rise, there was a welcome flatter part of the wall as it rounded the big old cistern. In that corner of the property there were huge old honeysuckle vines that grew up and over the wall. Scrambling our way through them, we'd often stop and pick the yellow blossoms, shaped like tiny trumpets, and pull out the inner stems to lick.

For a while the wall was fairly flat, riding along the top of the hill, where the original house had stood. The biggest challenge was when we came to the main entrance to the property, with its colorful Mexican tiles spelling LA ATALAYA. It soared up from the wall and into an arch several feet above the wrought iron gates that in our mother's day welcomed guests to the estate. On the very top of the arch we would pause for breath and look out over Serpentine Drive as it circled around outside the wall, and take in the breathtaking panoramas to the east and west, before we carefully climbed down the other side and proceeded on our way along the wall.

Soon we were facing the most challenging part of wall-walking, the descent. There was no way around it. If we retraced our steps and went back the way we came, we would still have to navigate the downward slope back to our starting point. Rather than going back we preferred to walk the entire circle. Where the wall started going down on the far side of the property the ground was craggy and forbidding on both sides, the rugged terrain covered with prickly weeds and small cactus, and maybe a rattlesnake or two hiding under the protruding rocks. So going down the hill was less like walking and more like scrambling and scooting along the wall, our feet in front, inching along on our bottoms, gripping the rough concrete with our hands, fighting gravity.

Describing it now, more than 50 years later, I find it hard to imagine that it sounds like anyone would choose to walk the wall, let alone do it year after year. But we were kids and it was a tradition, leaving memories of adventure and fun that I carry in my body as well as my mind.

Once we finally made it to the bottom of the hill, there was a long flat stretch of wall, running alongside the slough on the outside, and where there had once been beautiful plantings and a stable on the inside. From there, only one more leg to the trip, another climb halfway up the property, back to where we had started. Exhausted, but exhilarated with our accomplishment, we'd head directly to the kitchen for glasses of cold water and probably a handful each of Oreos. It took almost all afternoon to walk the wall, and we'd be pretty worn out and done with it.

Until next time, of course.

Throughout it all, the wall has stood proud, defining and protecting the land, with its cluster of Torrey pines and its rattlesnakes, holding the memories of fortunes made and lost, and families wondering, who will care for her when we're gone?

Let me take you back, to the beginning.

Chapter 1

How It All Started

Coy Burnett, the man who would become my grandfather, wasn't born rich. Unlike his children to come, he did not attend private boarding schools nor have governesses from Germany or Black nannies called nurses. His father didn't own a big company, and his clothes weren't hand-made in Paris, like his daughter Valentine's wardrobe of exquisitely stitched silk dresses designed for a one-year-old little girl to live like a princess, at least for a little while.

No, there was no silver spoon. Like most of our ancestors, Coy had a humble beginning. His family had traveled west and settled in McCook, Nebraska, where he was born in the late 1880s. In the eleventh grade Coy got a job cleaning the stables of the show horses belonging to W. R. Starr, a prominent attorney in Red Willow County. The attorney was

Young Coy Burnett (right) with his older brother William, wearing "M" caps, perhaps for McCook Senior High

impressed with Coy's ability to handle the prize horses, but beyond that he was drawn to the young man's intelligence and ability to perform whatever tasks were assigned to him. So Starr encouraged Coy to learn shorthand and court reporting, and soon made a place for him at his law office.

Coy accepted, and found that he had a good mind for the law. He worked for Starr preparing briefs and other documents, researching law and legal precedents. After he graduated from high school, Coy continued to work for a year in Starr's firm before he left McCook for the School of Law at the University of Nebraska in Lincoln. He stayed at the law school for only two semesters.

Already working in a law office in Lincoln, and impatient to get on with his career, Coy left school. And from then on, just as he had learned to handle horses by working with them, Coy Burnett learned the law by practicing it. He took a room in a boarding house in Lincoln and began working full time for the Strode and Strode law firm.

In 1909, with one year of post-high-school education, Coy took the Nebraska State Bar exam, and was examined orally by the Justices of the Supreme Court of Nebraska.

A few weeks later, the notification came to the boarding house: Coy Burnett had passed the exam. However, admission to the bar would be delayed. It would have to wait, the notification read, until he "reached his majority," turning 21.

A few months later, the second notice arrived. He was official, admitted to the bar by the Supreme Court on December 15, 1909, his 21st birthday.

One of the clients Coy represented at the Strode firm was the Standard Bridge Company of Omaha, then the most powerful group in the bridge and construction industry in the Midwest. When the Standard Bridge Company expanded into the timber business in the Columbia River Valley, litigation arose in connection with lumber properties there. In February of 1911, at the age of 22, Coy was sent to Portland, Oregon by the Strode firm to take charge of that litigation.

One afternoon during the trial, Coy had to ask the judge for a short continuance, so he could take that state's bar exam. He was permanently admitted to the bar by the Supreme Court of Oregon on April 23, 1912.

Coy liked Portland so much that he stayed. After doing litigation work for two prestigious Portland law firms, he opened his own practice, where his work consisted largely of trying cases for other attorneys. His own clients included the Southern Pacific Railroad in Oregon, the Pacific-Marine Iron Works, the United States Fidelity and Guaranty Company, the Columbia Shipbuilding Company, the Supple-Ballin Shipyards, and several businesses owned by Helwig Smith, mother of Alfred Smith, who was then governor of New York and would later become the Democratic candidate for President of the United States. It was at the Supple-Ballin Shipyards that he met Fred Ballin, who would become an important influence in his life.

Things were going well. In 1916, five years after his arrival in Portland, Coy bought and registered his first car, a Cadillac. It would be the first of many he would own.

It isn't clear where he found the time, but Coy did have a personal life. He had met Mildred Kingsbury, a fellow Nebraskan, and found in her not only a marital partner but a close associate in all matters, business and personal. Mildred was a little older. After attending the university she had left Nebraska and gone to Long Beach, in Southern California, to live with her younger sister Maud and work as a bookkeeper.

Maybe Coy and Mildred met at the university in Nebraska, but all that's known for sure about their early days as a couple is that they married in 1915. They were never the type to gather the grandkids around to tell their sweet story, so the details of my grandparents' relationship remain unknown to me. But marry they did, and Mildred moved to Portland, where she was a quiet colleague in Coy's legal practice. "I read transcripts, briefs, records, and wrote notes analyzing them, during all his trial work," she later wrote.

Mildred never liked Portland, complaining of the cold and the gray weather. But there they were. Their first child was born in Portland in 1916, the same year Coy bought his first Cadillac. They had a little girl, but that didn't change their plan to assign to the infant Mildred's maiden name, so the newborn was christened with the unlikely, and distinctly unfeminine, name of Kingsbury, later shortened to the nickname King.

Coy was busy with his practice and business ventures, and Mildred was busy at home and behind the scenes. World War I came along and the draft of 1917 and 1918. Coy registered but was never called to serve.

With his natural affinity for all things legal, Coy seemed to be destined for a long and successful career as an attorney. But life had other plans. Still, his legal experience is what led Coy to his ultimate destiny. His knowledge of the law and his audacity in tackling the unfamiliar would serve him faithfully throughout his long life.

It was in Oregon that he worked on an early antitrust case in the developing cement industry and met two men with a proposal to buy an old cement plant, but not for making cement. And it's in Portland that Coy Burnett hesitantly entered into their limited partnership, taking the chance that would make him a driving force in a place nearly a thousand miles away, the up-and-coming city of Los Angeles.

To understand my grandparents' story and how they got to Del Mar and built their estate, La Atalaya, requires a look back first at the history of Southern California and then also at the history of cement.

Chapter 2

The City of Angels

Southern California, with its diverse topography and Mediterranean climate, has been home to human ancestors for many thousands of years, enjoying its mild climate and rich natural resources. European exploration and settlement of the "New" World in the 17tth and 18th centuries led to Spain claiming a large amount of territory in what is now Mexico, calling it New Spain.

But attempts to colonize the indigenous people to the north, in what the Spaniards called Alta California, had all failed. Threatened by other countries' exploration efforts in the area, Spain asked the Roman Catholic Church to send priests, to build mission churches and convert the indigenous people to Christianity.

Of course, this was at least as much a strategy to enhance Spain's control over the natives' lives as it was to save their souls. Still, growing up in California in the 1950s, we kids learned about "Father" Serra and the history of the California missions the same way we were taught to think about Christopher Columbus – that they were courageous European forefathers who discovered and civilized our homeland.

Spain had three kinds of settlements in Alta California: mission (religious), presidio (military), and pueblo (town). The first mission was located not far north of Baja California; San Diego de Alcalá was erected in 1769, as was the first presidio.

The first pueblo was built farther north, near San Jose. The second pueblo, its name debated among historians, was officially founded on September 4, 1781. Whether it's El Pueblo de Nuestra Señora la Reina de los Ángeles de Porciúncula ("the town of our lady the Queen of Angels of the little Portion") or, more succinctly, El Pueblo de la Reyna de los Angeles ("the town of the Queen of Angels"), the name was a big one for a small settlement – 11 families, 40-some people. Whatever the full name, the large geographical basin, bisected by the Los Angeles River, encircled by mountains on three sides with the ocean to the west, would soon come to be known simply as Los Angeles.

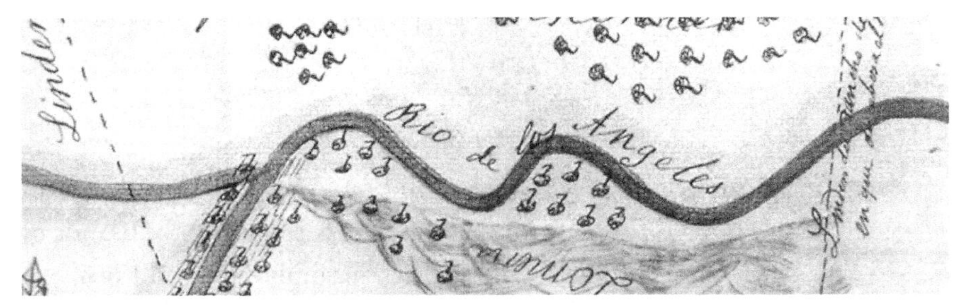

An early map of the Los Angeles River basin

As the native people had done for thousands of years, the settlers depended on the river for water, building a system of reservoirs and open ditches to irrigate nearby fields. By the 1850s, drawn to the kinder climate and developing opportunities there, people began to migrate to southern California from the Midwest and East Coast. But as the population grew, so did the need for water and, not for the last time in its history, Los Angeles began to experience water shortages.

Without more water the city couldn't become the major American metropolis envisioned by the movers and shakers of early L. A. A drought in the early 1900s added a sense of urgency to finding more water. The Los Angeles Board of Public Works began searching for such a source and a way to bring the water – somehow – to the semi-arid area.

By 1906 Los Angeles had secured a deed to water from the Owens Valley on the eastern side of the Sierras. The City began making plans to build a massive aqueduct system to take water from the Owens River and transport it all the way to L. A., more than 200 miles away.

The building of the Los Angeles Owens River Aqueduct, with its miles and miles of tunnels, canals, pipes and ditches, would require massive amounts of materials. Early planners knew concrete was to be the primary construction material, and concrete required cement. On September 9, 1906, the *Los Angeles Recorder* reported that a final decision had been made: Los Angeles would produce its own cement and, it was hoped, save the city millions of dollars. The building of a municipal cement plant in the Tehachapi Mountains northeast of Los Angeles was one of the first steps in the water project.

Why there? Not only did the mountains have plenty of the high-quality limestone and clay needed to construct the Aqueduct, but also the location was close to the geographic center of the project. So a plant was erected in the remote mountains, and alongside it was built a small settlement – basic houses, a bunkhouse and mess hall, a general store and a post office, for the workers and their families. When it was completed in 1908, the plant and adjacent town were named Aqueduct, a name that was changed to Monolith soon after, when a large deposit of limestone, an indispensable component of cement, was discovered nearby. The Monolith plant would operate continuously from the time it was completed in 1908 until the L. A. water project was done.

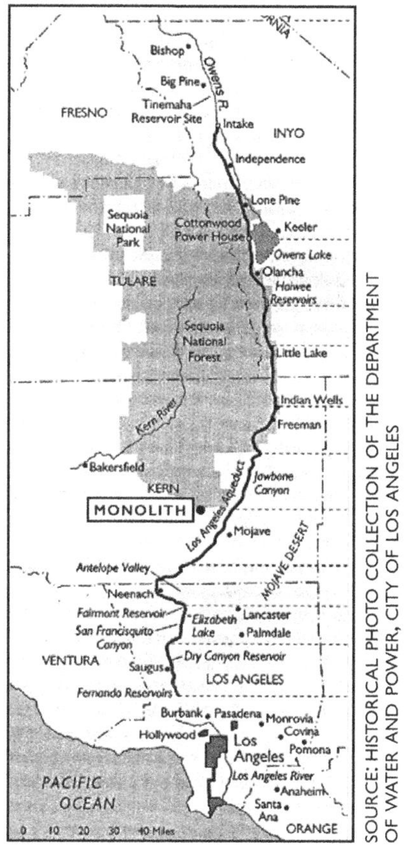

SOURCE: HISTORICAL PHOTO COLLECTION OF THE DEPARTMENT OF WATER AND POWER, CITY OF LOS ANGELES

A 1908 map showing the route of the Los Angeles Aqueduct, with a label added to show the Monolith cement plant, well placed along the way.

Manufacturing its own cement was only one of the ways Los Angeles saved money in building this massive project. One of the cost-saving measures, like the challenge of early water shortages, foreshadowed issues that would plague Los Angeles again: Superintendent Mulholland's so-called "low-wage policy." The immigrants who built the Aqueduct may have been drawn to the steady pay and equal opportunity, but most of them were undocumented, and therefore willing to work for lower wages.

This raised great controversy, and in 1913 a state bill was proposed banning undocumented workers from California Public Works projects. Opponents of the bill claimed that 90 percent of the workers on the project were foreign born and not naturalized, and quoted Mulholland

SOURCE: EASTERN CALIFORNIA MUSEUM

The town of Monolith (at first called Aqueduct) began as a factory making cement for the Los Angeles Aqueduct project and a camp for the people who worked at the factory.

as saying that the Los Angeles Aqueduct would have been too expensive to build otherwise. While the divisive debate raged on in the capitol in Sacramento, the citizens of Los Angeles enjoyed the fruits of the low-paid labor of undocumented workers.

In an echo of the legions of enslaved men who built the Roman aqueducts over 2,000 years earlier, almost 4,000 workers labored at top speed to complete the L. A. Aqueduct project. The work itself was dangerous and the weather was extreme out there in the Mojave Desert and Owens Valley, severe heat in the summer, freezing temperatures in the winter.

The workforce was diverse; most workers were Greek, Bulgarian, Serbian, Montenegrin, Swiss, Mexican and American Indian. Unlike those who labored for the Romans, they were free men. Pay was $2.25 per day, plus food and shelter. Healthcare benefits were rare in those days, but the full-time workers on the Aqueduct project were offered full medical coverage for $1 a month.

Unlike the Romans, the builders of this Aqueduct had help – for instance, the new tractors that could haul heavy materials up steep slopes. It's said that Project Superintendent William Mulholland, on watching an initial demonstration of one of these machines, claimed "It crawls like a caterpillar." The name stuck, and with Caterpillars and other modern equipment assisting the wagons and mule teams, the workers set records for miles tunneled and canals laid.

The Aqueduct was a really big deal. In spite of the new machinery and huge labor force, it took seven years to build. When it was done it was 233 miles long, the largest single water project and the longest aqueduct in the world. There are old postcards depicting different stages of its construction.

The Aqueduct would channel water from the snowcapped Sierra Mountains and the Owens River through tunnels, canals, and pipes onto a spillway, where it flowed into the San Fernando Valley. Adventurous travelers drove off in their new roadsters to trace its rugged path. The whole country marveled at the accomplishment, at the time considered to be the second greatest engineering feat of the modern era, topped only by the building of the Panama Canal.

The City of Angels got her water. Gathered at the dedication ceremony on November 5, 1913, a large crowd watched, cheering loudly as the first gallons flowed through the Aqueduct.

SOURCE: HISTORICAL PHOTO COLLECTION OF THE DEPARTMENT OF WATER AND POWER, CITY OF LOS ANGELES

The tractors used to help complete the Elizabeth Lake Tunnel in the Los Angeles Aqueduct project were among the first "caterpillars" ever built. The tunnel cut through the Coast Range to make it possible to deliver water from the Eastern Sierra.

Postcards published by the Benham Indiam Trading Company between 1910 and 1915, showing construction techniques used to tunnel through a mountain range to bring water from the Owens River to Los Angeles. Left: *Timbering was used in tunneling through soft rock and dangerous slips.* Right: *When two tunnel headings met, the men shook hands through the hole.*

SOURCE: LOS ANGELES AQUEDUCT DIGITAL PLATFORM, UCLA LIBRARY SPECIAL COLLECTIONS

But the new water transport system wasn't unanimously popular. Violent protests in the Owens Valley followed the completion of the project. Today it's acknowledged that robbing the river valley and surrounding areas of their water destroyed the terrain, and ruined some communities even as it built others elsewhere.

Still, many consider the Los Angeles Aqueduct to be one of the top 10 public works projects of the 20th century. It's difficult to imagine what Los Angeles, now the second largest city in the United States, would be without water. And it's harder to imagine what the U. S. would be without L. A.

When the Aqueduct was finished, the Monolith plant was closed, and L. A. was presented with the quandary of what to do with a municipal cement plant, which had now served its function – demolish it? sell it? keep it as a municipal facility?

With its new source of water, Los Angeles was growing fast and so were its citizens' needs. Public works included municipal buildings for the ever increasing population, and bridges and roads for the ever increasing automobiles. No problem – the City could not only build the facilities, but also make the materials to do so.

In 1915 it was decided that the City would lease the Monolith plant to the County, which would maintain it as a public work. The plant in the mountains was reopened, and for a time the County of Los Angeles was in the cement-making business.

However, the enthusiasm over the reopening of Monolith was matched by a determined opposition, and soon legal action was brought against the City and County of Los Angeles, charging that the manufacture of cement and concrete was outside the rights and responsibilities of a municipality. The case made it to the California Supreme Court, which upheld the opposition to the municipal plant. Once again, in early 1918, the plant at Monolith was closed down.

What does all this have to do with Coy and Mildred Burnett and their move to Southern California? The answer to that question begins with two words: *portland cement.*

Chapter 3

Portland Cement – and Potash

At first glance, the topic of cement is as gray and dry as the powdered substance itself. But dig a bit deeper into that bag of ground limestone and clay, and you'll find history, drama and intrigue lurking within its gritty interior. In *Making the Modern World: Materials and Dematerialization,* historian Vaclav Smil notes that concrete is "the most important material in terms of sheer mass in our civilization." And to make concrete requires cement, the sticky stuff that glues together the world.

Concrete – typically, cement mixed with water, rock and sand – has played a critical role throughout human history. The Romans built extensively with their own form of concrete; the tall ruins of their ancient arches and aqueducts still stand, proudly proclaiming the strength and durability of their building material. But that was only a couple of millennia ago. The Nabataea traders, Bedouins, were building with early forms of concrete even before the Romans.

There are many varieties of cement. Concrete's ingredients, including cement, tell a story about the people who built with it, what they did, and what they had on hand. In constructing the buildings on the sugar estates in the Danish West Indies, for instance, chunks of rock from the volcanic islands were combined with coral from the ocean and cemented together with a mixture of ground seashells and, thanks to all that sugar cane, thick molasses.

Mixed in with the rock and coral was another ingredient – chunks of broken yellow bricks, originally used as ballast on the slave ships that for more than 200 years brought hundreds of shiploads of enslaved Africans (and yellow bricks) to the New World through the West Indies in the sad history of the transatlantic slave trade. As a building material this concrete may have been crude by modern standards, but many of the sugar mills are still at least partially standing today.

As concrete evolved in the early 20th century, builders widely favored "portland" cement, which has its own story to tell. Portland cement was developed when an English bricklayer, in search of an alternative to the type of cement used originally by the Romans, was inspired to burn powdered lime (calcium carbonate, CaCO3) and clay in his kitchen stove. He was delighted with the result, and patented the formula in 1824. The concrete made with the new cement resembled a type of prized building stone quarried off the coast of England, on the Island of Portland, and thus the inventor called his invention "portland" cement.

A century later, in Coy Burnett's time, portland cement was far finer and stronger than that original concoction. Mixed into concrete, portland cement was strong, resilient, and durable enough to hold together whole modern cities. The early 1900s were a time of change, a time of rapid urbanization and industrialization in the United States. Cities were booming and the automobile was becoming commonplace thanks to mass production, and that required new roads and highways, new dams, new bridges.

Gray and dull perhaps, but where would we be without portland cement? Driving on dirt or cobblestone roads, crossing rivers on ferries, living in buildings constructed of molasses and seashells, or wattle and daub – sticks woven and pasted together with a sticky mix of wet soil, straw, and animal dung. The world we live in is held together with concrete, and 95 percent of concrete is made with portland cement.

Besides being a time of building, the early years of the 20th century were also a time of widespread reform, in response to the greed and corruption of the so-called "gilded" era that ended the 19th century. It was a time of trust-busting fat monopolies and bringing down crooked political machines.

In 1916 in Portland, Coy Burnett, along with John Logan and I. N. Smith, agreed to represent Aman Moore, one of the first cement engineers in the United States, in an anti-trust case. Moore was bringing conspiracy charges against fellow executives within the Oregon Portland Cement Company as well as 14 other cement companies, alleging that, among many acts of misconduct, they had conspired to fix prices and take over or ruin the Oregon company.

The case went before a Federal Grand Jury. Stories about the trial dominated the headlines in the *Portland Oregonian* for months, reporting that the hearing was "enlivened by sharp skirmishes" between the attorneys. Quotes from Coy Burnett present him as confident and self-assured: He had it all figured out.

By now Coy had multiple irons in the fire. As the attorney for prominent local businesses he had come to know Fred Ballin. Primarily invested in shipbuilding, Ballin wanted to expand. After the dust settled on the anti-trust case, Ballin and Aman Moore approached Coy with a business proposition. They had obtained the rights to certain patents for making potash, and planned to open a facility to do so. They proposed that Coy take a one-third interest in the new business, potentially very profitable.

Potash is a critical component in manufacturing, and was being used in making soap and glass as long ago as 500 AD; it was also used in fertilizer. Originally it was made by burning wood, using water to leach the chemicals from the ashes, and then boiling away the water. The leftover white residue was called "pot ash," and the term "potash" was then used to refer to the natural potassium salt ore deposits that were discovered within the earth. Potassium got its name from potash.

Coy was impressed with Moore and Ballin's knowledge of the industry, including the vast amount of information they had gathered from a tour of potash facilities around the United States. They told Coy that, based on their research, they had located the optimal setting for their potash venture: a closed cement plant in Southern California. Though reluctant to take on such a big project, Coy began to warm to the notion of a new challenge, and Ballin, Moore and Burnett entered into a formal agreement to, according to Coy's autobiographical notes, "associate themselves together for the purpose of investigating and perhaps entering into the potash and similar industries." Unsure he wanted to be involved in the actual operation of the business, of which he had no experience, Coy opted to serve as counsel and secretary, while continuing his Portland law practice.

Chapter 4

Wheeling and Dealing

The Great War was over. The influenza epidemic that followed it had killed more people than the world war, but it too was over. At the dawn of the 1920s, things were looking up, and life was changing. The 19th Amendment had passed, prohibiting denial or abridgment of the right to vote on account of sex.

In 1920 it was Coy Burnett's job to make a deal with the City of Los Angeles to buy a shut-down cement plant. Coy had just turned 31. He was a successful attorney and an influential businessman, a husband and father who could have stayed comfortably settled in Oregon. But he was on the move, traveling fast.

On April 23, 1920, in a meeting between the Board of Public Service Commissioners of the City of Los Angeles and Coy Burnett, representing his associates in Oregon, negotiations were finalized. The deal was signed, handshakes were exchanged, and the rights to the possession and use of the Monolith cement plant and related properties were acquired pursuant to a five-year lease agreement.

A company was quickly incorporated, and the United States Potash Company was born, its first task a daunting one: to recondition the worn-out plant and facilities and get them operating again, in order to make potash.

Right from the start, things didn't go smoothly. It turned out that while the City was holding its breath hoping for a buyer, and Coy and his associates were hatching schemes to get a good deal on the Monolith plant, the bottom fell out of the potash market, perhaps because potash was being produced more cheaply in Germany. By the time they'd shaken hands on the deal, potash prices had collapsed and with them all the plans of the U. S. Potash Company. Just born, the new company needed to reinvent itself.

When you suddenly find yourself with a cement plant on your hands, what do you do? Make cement of course. The new company turned its efforts to the production of portland cement, and on August 8, 1920 the U. S. Potash Company rolled out its first barrel.

The owners of U. S. Potash may have breathed a sigh of relief as they filled their first barrel of cement, but they knew they would have to do more than manufacture it. It was true that Los Angeles was growing rapidly and would need plenty of cement to keep doing so. However, there were already four other cement companies in the area, and all of them were closer to the city than Monolith. Cement is heavy, and transporting it is the greatest expense in its marketing. The plant in the Tehachapi Mountains was 117 rail miles from the city. Monolith needed something special to compete – a better product, better service.

In October of 1920, the U. S. Potash Company acquired the exclusive license to manufacture and sell Plastic Waterproof Cement, patented only two years earlier. This specialty product would prove to have advantages over regular portland cement in terms of plasticity, setting strength and workability, and eventually it would become a trademark of the U. S. Potash Company. But it would take time for the new product to catch on, and the company was scrambling to keep ahead of the financial challenges. The year 1920 ended with the United States Potash Company in the red.

It wasn't just the external forces that challenged the company in those early years. There were shakeups within the company as well. Fred Ballin, as president, had decided Aman Moore wasn't quite who he seemed to be, and began to have doubts about having Moore stay involved. Around that same time, the Pacific Portland Cement Company offered $1,000,000 to purchase the lease to the Monolith plant. While he wasn't ready to sell, this got Ballin thinking. He approached Coy about buying out Moore's portion. This would include rights to the waterproof cement patent and being given the first chance to buy Ballin out, should he choose to sell in the future. The offer was conditional on Coy taking over the day-to-day running of the plant. So the self-taught lawyer from McCook, Nebraska decided to take on a whole new profession.

Up to this time, Coy had been commuting the 900-plus miles back and forth between his law practice and family in Portland, and the cement business near Los Angeles. That needed to change. Whether it was the golden business opportunity for Coy or the golden climate for Mildred, or both, they would soon leave Portland and head south to establish a new home.

By the summer of 1921, their name no longer relevant, the U. S. Potash Company reinvented itself as the Monolith Portland Cement Company. Fred Ballin was still president but Aman Moore was out, and Coy Burnett, Vice President and General Manager, was now in charge of all operations of a remote cement plant in the mountains outside Los Angeles. Quite a contrast to small-town Nebraska.

A red "M" on the bags and barrels identified the product of the newly branded Monolith Portland Cement Company.

For one thing, right from the start Monolith was a culturally diverse workplace, where the primarily Hispanic, American Indian and white folks, almost all men, worked side by side. The men labored long hard hours and relied on one another in the demanding, sometimes dangerous, industry of making cement. Isolated in the mountains, many of them lived with their families in the company town of Monolith.

Years later folks would recall that, in spite of the small size of the place, families were divided by the railroad tracks: Mexican and Indian to the north, white to the south. Still, perhaps being isolated together in the small town enhanced a sense of community.

In 2009, Jon Hammond, a reporter for the *Tehachapi News*, characterized the history of the workplace culture at Monolith as "equality covered in dust," saying disagreements at the plant were personal, not based on ethnic or cultural differences. "When you're tired, dusty, and sweating in the heat or shivering from the cold, you care more about your co-workers' reliability than their social background."

Monolith would be known for many things throughout its long history making cement, but surely the most remarkable was that it moved influential songwriter and steel guitarist John Fahey to write an instrumental entitled "The Portland Cement Factory at Monolith, California," first heard on his 1967 album *Days Have Gone By.* Surely not many cement plants can claim to have inspired music.

But Monolith was no ordinary cement plant. It had already had several incarnations by the time Coy Burnett, now in charge of daily operations, had joined the multicultural workers at the plant late in 1920. He had closed his practice in Portland, and he and Mildred had packed up their household and four-year-old daughter, Kingsbury, and left Oregon and their old life behind. With another baby on the way, they traveled south, to Los Angeles, the city growing rapidly among the citrus groves.

At this point they had never heard of the little seaside village of Del Mar, but like a siren luring Odysseus, she was already calling out to them with her natural beauty and the music of the sea.

Chapter 5

Del Mar Before the Burnetts

As you stand at the mouth of the San Dieguito Lagoon where it opens into the Pacific, with the river valley at your back and the warm sand between your toes, your face is warmed by the last heat of the afternoon sun as it sinks slowly toward the horizon and casts shadows on the hills that rise along the coast. It's easy to see why so many have found their way to this beautiful land, going back thousands of years, long before it was called Del Mar.

The city of Del Mar today extends from the Los Peñasquitos Lagoon on the south, to the San Dieguito Lagoon on the north. It extends inland from the beaches and coastal bluffs of the Pacific Ocean on the west, up a range of hills to the east. Cliffs with layers of fossils on the southern end of the area reveal the history of ancient lagoons.

The area has had many names through the years. While some are lost to time, others have quite a story. In the 1840s a small farming community called Cordero, north of the Peñasquitos lagoon, was given a new name – Weed. While the renaming might not have been the best marketing strategy, it was intended to honor William Weed, a local man, a respected and well loved fellow citizen who owned a large amount of land in the area. Weed was college-educated and spoke several languages. The town's name was a touching tribute surely, but it was doomed to a fairly short life. The lovely town center of Weed was made up of two houses, a barn, a post office and an official stagecoach stop on the El Camino Real route.

The bluffs along the ocean west of Weed were christened in 1882, when Theodore Loop and his young wife, Ella, came to town. Loop was the engineer and contractor for completion of the California Southern Railroad connecting San Diego north to the San Bernardino Valley. Legend has it that when Loop arrived he declared that he'd "found the most attractive place on the entire coast." Theodore and Ella set up a tent city on the beach, and Ella dubbed it "Del Mar," after a popular poem of the time, Bayard Taylor's "The Fight of Paso Del Mar." The name stuck, but when the railroad opened in 1883, the "flag" stop was not in Del Mar, but in Weed.

That would soon change. Around the same time the Loops were setting up their tent city, a Texan land speculator named Jacob Shell Taylor purchased – sight unseen – the rancho of Los Peñasquitos. Once he arrived to check out his new property, Taylor started buying up more land, and talking other landowners into shared ownership. It was all part of a grand scheme to create, subdivide and develop Del Mar into a seaside resort. By 1885 Jacob Taylor owned or had a partnership controlling almost 350 acres of prime oceanfront property, all for less than $2,000 in gold coin.

A post office was built, and in 1885 a train depot, at the intersection of 9th Street and Railroad Avenue. The train started coming through, and efforts to establish the large resort went forward, full steam ahead. Taylor's luxury resort hotel, the Casa Del Mar, opened in 1886, with band concerts and a speech from the governor of California. It was the "most elegantly sited and commodious hotel on the Coast between Los Angeles and San Diego," according to its advertisements, with its 30 rooms complete with "all modern improvements including electric bells, gas, baths, etc." There was even a dance pavilion on the beach.

Casa Del Mar was a great success and made Del Mar a popular destination, but not for long. In 1890, only four years after its grand opening, and after two years of unusual rains and flooding in the area, the Casa Del Mar burned to the ground. People who had moved to Del Mar to work at the resort, and those who had bought land in the area just a few years before, began to leave. It was unusual for more than a couple of people to arrive at the depot on any train, and the run-down buildings and empty houses gathered around the station were a sad testimonial to Del Mar having seen better days. By the turn of the century, Del Mar had only about a hundred residents.

But the little town was resilient and would bounce back. In 1891 Henry Keller, who had inherited from his developer father the 20,000 acres we now call Malibu and then sold the land, joined fellow millionaire William G. Kerckhoff and Henry E. Huntington, railroad and empire builder, to found the South Coast Land Company. They intended to buy up the mostly undeveloped land along the Pacific coast south of Los Angeles and develop it.

It was a huge endeavor. The plan was to develop whole towns along the coast, linking them together with the Pacific Electric Railway, Huntington's massive electric railway system, which was already up and running in Los Angeles. They dreamed of ultimately harnessing hydro-electric power in the region.

There was a 10-mile stretch of coast north of San Diego with some beautiful beaches that the South Coast Land Company believed had real potential, particularly as stops for the electric Red Car. In 1905 Del Mar was the first city to be developed.

The South Coast Land Company had plans for Del Mar that put Colonel Taylor's vision in its place: a new, grander luxury hotel with ocean views; a pier extending a thousand feet out into the ocean for fishing and strolling; an enormous enclosed heated saltwater pool called a "plunge"; a powerhouse to provide electricity for the hotel and nearby properties, and to pump and heat the seawater for the Warm Water Plunge; and of course, a Red Car station for Huntington's railway. The resort was to be elegant, understated, tasteful.

When the Stratford Inn opened in 1909, modeled after Shakespeare's England, the Tudor style of architecture was established as setting just the right tone for the new resort. A tiny half-timbered pseudo-Elizabethan town sprang up around the hotel, complete with a carriage house, a bath house, cottages and shops. Breezy Del Mar, with its perfect climate and soft sand beaches, became a popular summer destination for Hollywood's silent film stars and others escaping the Los Angeles heat.

South Coast Land Company had big plans for Del Mar.

Henry Keller was not as involved as his partner Kerckhoff in the hotel and other developments in Del Mar, preferring to stay in the Los Angeles area. But Henry's sister Caroline was drawn to the hilly village by the sea. She and her husband, E. J. Schafer, searched for property on which to build a cottage. They finally found it, at the northernmost end of the ridge of the Del Mar hill, with an expansive view of the Pacific.

From the crest of the hill, where Caroline and her husband planned to build, ridges and ravines bisected the land as it ran down to the beaches and the sea to the west, and, on the eastern side of the hill, down to deep ravines and the San Dieguito River valley. Dramatic rock outcroppings among the scrub brush and Torrey pines, the fragrant smell of eucalyptus trees and wild sage, and a wide view of the sun setting over the ocean made the property at the top of the hill, if wild and undeveloped, very appealing indeed.

They had the land cleared and built a cottage for $40,000, in the Craftsman style so popular in Southern California then. The wide porch, dormers, and deep overhanging eaves with their faint Asian influence fit the house's Arts and Crafts esthetic: simple but pleasing design, of wood and other natural materials, built with exquisite craftsmanship.

The South Coast Land Company published a brochure promoting the wisdom of joining fellow citizens (with means) and buying land in the up and coming resort town of Del Mar, California. Caroline Keller Schafer was listed in the brochure as a proud property owner, along with 50 other "prominent Southern California people."

But Del Mar was in for another roller coaster ride, as the South Coast Land Company's scheme was thwarted. E. H. Harriman and the Southern Pacific Railroad jumped the gun on Huntington's Red Line, and the electric train was ousted. Instead of serving the Pacific Electric Railway, the partially built brick train depot in Del Mar was completed, Tudor-style, as a stop between Los Angeles and San Diego for the Santa Fe Railroad.

The dreams of establishing and selling hydroelectric power fell away along with the dream of an electric train, and the South Coast Land Company no longer had a foothold in Southern California. Plans changed, and some of the 51 people listed in the glossy brochure left before they ever built on their properties.

Caroline Keller Schafer stayed on for a while. Whether she enjoyed the cottage on the hill in Del Mar as much as she had hoped is unknown. The only record is from 1924, when she sold it, complete with furnishings, household goods, even the china dishes and silverware. And, of course, the view.

The buyers? Mildred Burnett of Los Angeles and her pale, recovering husband, Coy, the cement company president fresh out of the shadows of convalescence at the Virginia Hotel in Long Beach.

Caroline and E. J. Schafer had a Craftsman-style house built on their lot. Later it became part of La Atalaya. The house is shown here in a photo from the 1930s.

Chapter 6

Granddaddy's Breakdown

A couple of years after the Burnetts moved south from Oregon to L. A., Fred Ballin made a decision. Having already sunk more than $600,000 into the leased Monolith plant, he decided to take the money and run.

Because of their previous agreement, Coy was given first crack at buying his partner out. Coy took out a loan of $1,000,000 from the Hellman National Bank, and after some negotiating he paid off Ballin and put the rest of the money into company funds. He now owned the controlling interest in the company, and on August 27, 1923 Coy Burnett was elected President of the Monolith Portland Cement Company, a position he would hold for nearly 50 years.

Smoking Room Stories

I remember that my cousin Dana, the son of Coy's daughter Anne, loved to pull us younger cousins aside and speculate about how Granddaddy got Monolith, whispering about the mysterious death of one of his partners, the suspicious circumstances behind our grandfather's rapid ascent to power in the cement business.

When visiting our grandparents' elegant home in Los Angeles during the 1950s and '60s, we cousins did not find it hard to believe that Dana's stories might be true. Especially when, walking past the dining room, with its dinner table that could be expanded to seat 30 to 40 people, we caught a glimpse through the door next to it, into Granddaddy's study.

Dark, wood-paneled and masculine, with leather-covered armchairs and an attached all black marble bathroom (the entire room – walls, floors, fixtures - black marble), the room seemed to match our grandfather's somber and rather forbidding character. It was called the Smoking Room, which somehow added to it an aura of being off-limits to us kids. When visiting our grandparents, we usually crept quickly past the Smoking Room door, but occasionally we were invited in.

Coy Burnett (center) and some of his cronies in the Smoking Room (August, 1948)

We went willingly, in spite of our pounding hearts. Because we knew that in the top left-hand drawer of his shiny mahogany desk, Granddaddy kept an inexhaustible supply of Clorets gum. While we watched, he'd take out one of the little boxes, always a fresh one, and ceremoniously remove the cellophane wrapper from the bright green and white cardboard packet. Opening the tiny tab on one end, he'd shake the little pillow-shaped rectangles of chewing gum into the palm of his hand and offer them to us. The gum was covered with a hard candy coating, bright green like the box. Sharply minty, it produced a satisfying crunch with the first bite.

When Coy became the company president, he started running things at Monolith his way. There were serious challenges in those early years, among them the perennial need for the literal mountains of raw materials to make cement. Aware that shells provide a useful supply of the gypsum needed in cement production to slow down the setting of the concrete, Coy decided Monolith should purchase a few uninhabited islands off the coast of Corpus Christi, Texas. But the directors of the Monolith Portland Cement Company voted down his decision.

Coy was apparently undeterred by this lack of support. Whether out of petulant stubbornness or brilliant business intuition, he scraped together the money, no doubt adding to his million-dollar debt, and purchased the islands anyway, in the name of Coy and Mildred Burnett. He was convinced this was the right choice. When oil was later found on Shamrock Island, Coy must have felt a terrific kind of gratification in this epic-like vindication of his dogged decisiveness so many years before.

But the thing that lingers on in family history about the conflict over Shamrock Island is the question of whether that, on top of his rapid rise to power, may have been the last straw in the mounting weight of Coy's ever increasing wealth, influence and responsibility.

While Los Angeles continued to build, and the Roaring Twenties got into full swing, Coy 's blood pressure skyrocketed over 300. Always driven and high-strung, he collapsed with a "nervous breakdown." Ultimately it would be the breakdown that brought my family to Del Mar. Without it, there would be no La Atalaya, no beautiful estate designed by a famous architect in the 1920s, no wall. But first Coy had to get back on his feet.

Mildred and Coy's doctor for many years was Verne R. Mason, a physician of some importance. Dr. Mason is credited with naming a newly identified illness, Sickle Cell Anemia, during his residency at Johns Hopkins. In the 1920s he came to Southern California, where he practiced and taught at the University of Southern California (USC), a school highly favored by my grandparents, particularly for its football team.

Dr. Mason was the long-term personal physician of Howard Hughes as well as Coy Burnett. It seems the good doctor was very good at keeping things private, a quality undoubtedly valued – perhaps required – by both men, privacy being a privilege of power.

But is it possible that the respected Verne Mason was the mastermind behind the bizarre medical treatment of my grandfather's physical and mental breakdown? The centerpiece of the treatment was the prescription of rest. Rest, that is, with a twist: It involved certain rituals, and was to take place in a very quiet, darkened space.

So Coy, Mildred, King and Anne moved from their home, one of a series of mansions they rented while living in Los Angeles, and temporarily took up residence in the Virginia Hotel in Long Beach. It was the early 1920s; maybe it was the influence of the relatively new science of psycho-

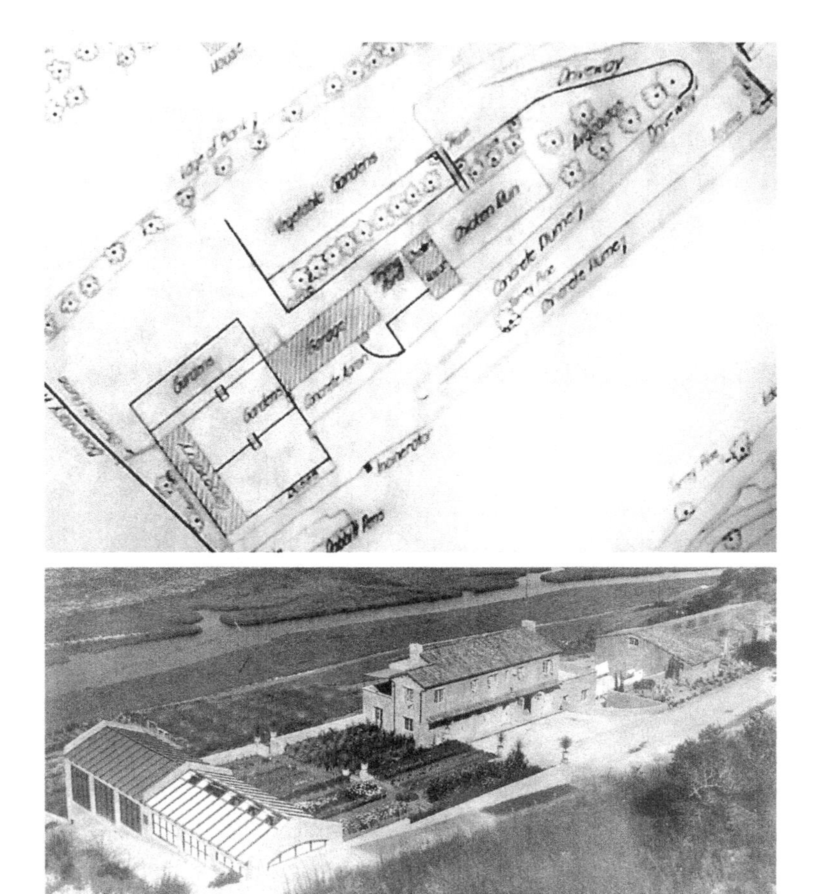

The Requa and Jackson architectural firm designed the mid-level buildings as part of a plan for the entire 23-acre walled estate. The mid-level buildings were the first to be constructed on the hillside property. (The architects' original map of the "Coy Burnett Property" was found many years later, rolled up, stored away and forgotten; a detail is shown here.)

Architectural Details: Spain and the Mediterranean, was published in 1926 by the Monolith Portland Cement Company, a beautiful boxed collection of black-and-white photographs in sections like "Houses – Country Type," "Buildings – City Type," "Street Facades and Entrances," "Balconies and Gates," "Roofs and Towers." The folio was donated free to architectural libraries and builders, ostensibly as a resource documenting authentic details, and all the while promoting the Mediterranean style of architecture, constructed with concrete "stucco," as most fitting for the area. It was the 1926 version of an infomercial.

And it worked. The folio was a success and had a second limited printing as a large book with an impressed pictorial faux leather hard cover. That was followed up with another trip, also funded by Monolith, by Requa, camera in hand, to North Africa and the Mediterranean, and another book was published in 1929.

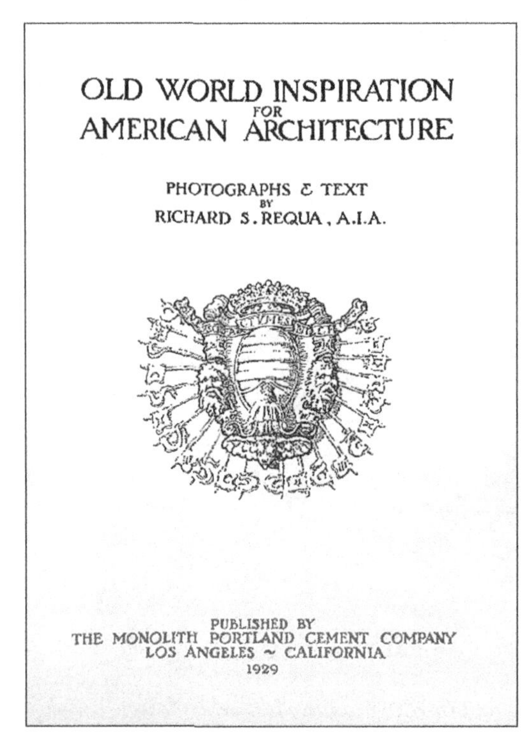
OLD WORLD INSPIRATION
FOR
AMERICAN ARCHITECTURE

PHOTOGRAPHS & TEXT
BY
RICHARD S. REQUA, A.I.A.

PUBLISHED BY
THE MONOLITH PORTLAND CEMENT COMPANY
LOS ANGELES ~ CALIFORNIA
1929

The title page (left) and a bookplate from the second limited-edition book sponsored by Monolith, with Richard Requa's photographs of North African and Mediterranean architecture.

And most important, at least to my family, was that folks who could afford it wanted a home designed in the Requa tradition, "authentic" Southern California, beautifully constructed to last forever from concrete made with Monolith cement. Coy and Mildred hadn't yet built their Requa-designed dream home, so the family was still living in Caroline's cottage, but there were big plans going forward.

It was only the late 1920s. Things were good. There was plenty of time.

Chapter 9

1929

The late Twenties was a swell time to be rich. Business was going great guns. With its waterproof cement selling steadily and its "good will" relationship with the City of Los Angeles keeping the plant working hard, Monolith was solidly in the black. Mildred and Coy were able to keep the estate in Del Mar, with its large staff, while maintaining a *pied-a-terre* in Los Angeles, which allowed them to avoid long separations when Coy was working. It was a fast-paced life. They were temporarily living at the Los Angeles Country Club in 1925 when Coy Jr. was born, perhaps so Mildred had access to better medical services.

The Burnett daughters, Kingsbury and Anne, always stayed in Del Mar when they were young, studying with their governesses, playing in the gardens. As teens they lived at Marlborough, an exclusive girls' boarding school in Los Angeles. Later in life King reflected, "I was the only one of my parents' children that they actually raised themselves."

But there were good times together as a whole family too. Even grand times. After Coy Jr.'s birth the family took several trips, including a voyage through the Panama Canal, with a stop in Cuba to tour a sugar plant. They went to Hawaii for five weeks in 1926, in part to look for sources of gypsum, used in making cement (Coy probably wrote off the trip); they liked it so much they went back the next year. Life was good. Those ocean voyages must have been something, with the steamer trunks and elegant staterooms, the children and servants, the luxury.

Mildred and Coy Jr.

Of course the Twenties weren't good for everyone. While the Burnetts were living at the country club and taking their children to exotic places, farmers were struggling to put food on their own tables. Cities and industry were growing, but most folks still lived in rural communities, and they were not living like Jay and Daisy Gatsby, or Coy and Mildred Burnett. The disparity between the rich and everybody else was mounting, The same year the average American was making $750 annually, automotive mogul Henry Ford reported a personal income of $14 million.

Such gaps offered fertile opportunities for corruption and crime. In Chicago it was the time of Al Capone and bloody gang violence, culminating on February 14th, 1929 in the shooting death of seven men known to associate with Irish gangster Bugs Moran. It became known as the St. Valentine's Day Massacre.

On that same day, in Los Angeles, at Good Samaritan Hospital, Mildred Kingsbury Burnett gave birth to a little girl. After avoiding it with her first two daughters, my grandmother finally conceded to her husband's desire to give a daughter his wife's first name, and the newborn baby was duly called Mildred. But her birth on a holiday with sweet traditions seemed to cry out for recognition. So she was named Mildred Valentine Burnett and she was known as Valentine, or Val, for the rest of her life.

Valentine's birth completed the Burnett family. It also changed the life of one of the staff, that of Houston's then wife Jessie, who was promoted

The staff at La Atalaya in 1930 included the cook, housemaids, and the younger children's nurses: Jessie, Valentine's nurse on the far left and Coy Jr.'s nurse, Elizabeth, on the far right.

from her job as housemaid to being the new baby's "nurse," or nanny. Valentine and Jessie joined Coy Jr. and his nurse, Elizabeth, and, along with the other staff and the older sisters and sometimes even their parents, they all lived together at La Atalaya.

Family trips remained a priority. When Mildred had become pregnant with Valentine in 1928 (four years after Coy Jr.'s birth, right on schedule), she and Coy considered it no reason to stop traveling. The plan to take a trip to Europe in the summer of 1929 proceeded undeterred. Baby Valentine was less than five months old when the family launched on their grand tour.

Just getting from Los Angeles to New York, where they boarded the passenger ship, must have been a small triumph, requiring several days' travel by train. With the family of six plus Jessie and Elizabeth, not to mention Coy's mother and Mildred's father, they made quite an entourage.

After crossing the Atlantic they spent several days in Paris and then continued on to Brussels, Berlin and finally Copenhagen, where my grandparents had business friends. King, a gangly boyish 13, enjoyed the trip a great deal, and later in life remembered fondly the family walks through the Bois du Boulogne and getting to go to the Folies Bergère, where she especially enjoyed the underwater act.

Jessie and Elizabeth often walked together, Jessie pushing Valentine's carriage and Elizabeth holding young Coy's hand as they strolled through the city streets, drawing the frankly curious stares of the Parisians as they watched this pair of striking young Black women with the elegant baby buggy and tow-headed little boy.

What was it like for Jessie, her promotion to caring for the new baby, this elegant travel? How had she felt entering the Burnett family and their small community of "staff"? What did she make of the Burnetts, Coy so forceful and certain, Mildred so remote, their children so separate? Was she shocked that the parents lived at the Ambassador Hotel or the L. A. Country Club, while their older daughters lived at boarding school and the servants raised their son and youngest daughter at the family estate in Del Mar?

Whatever her opinions were, she kept them to herself. Instead she remembered those as the "days when I was having fun," telling stories about how she sometimes carried a bottle of Champagne in the baby's diaper bag. Back at the hotel, after they'd gotten the children to sleep, she and Elizabeth would have a glass or two, pulling back the heavy curtains of their hotel window and gazing at the Parisian streets below.

Jessie, with her sleek head of crimped hair and slightly exotic features, was very fashionable in those days, being the recipient of Mildred's hand-me-downs. And these were some serious secondhand clothes, as Mildred 's main indulgence was stylish, beautifully made clothing. She needed to get rid of last year's designs to make room in her closets for this season's line, and Jessie was happy to take the "dated" apparel off her hands.

What might the pretty young woman from Little Rock have been thinking as she boarded the glamorous ocean liner to travel across the Atlantic, or when she walked through the streets of some of the great capitals of Europe wearing an exquisitely cut Art Deco dress, her hair in perfect waves made slick and fragrant with pomade? Quite a contrast to her life in Arkansas, living with her older brother Cecil and their grandmother in a series of small rentals.

The Burnetts' excursion to Europe at the zenith of the Roaring Twenties was a once-in-a-lifetime experience, and not just for Jessie. Evidence of the exotic elegance of that trip is left behind in the wardrobe made by hand in Paris for infant Valentine, a collection of nearly twenty little Art Deco–styled silk dresses and coats, for the tiniest of flappers, each with exquisite needlework – embroidery, smocking or cutwork, every tiny buttonhole

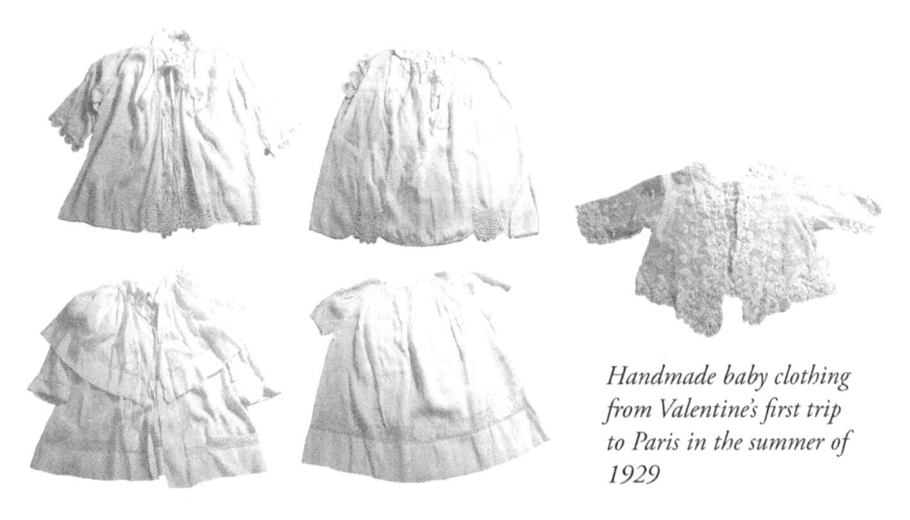

Handmade baby clothing from Valentine's first trip to Paris in the summer of 1929

Valentine Burnett

perate climate or blue skies in Del Mar one bit. The ocean kept sparkling to the west, the waves continued to break on the shore, and the property remained an endless source of fun and adventure. As far as Valentine and her brother, Coy, were concerned the greatest hardship of those years would be the absence of other kids, and doing their Calvert School work.

Mildred's sister Maud – for reasons lost to time, everyone called her Aunty Too – was forced by frail health to leave her career as a teacher. She lived with the Burnetts for much of her life, and during Valentine's childhood she lived in Del Mar. Living with Aunty Too and Jessie and the other staff, the younger Burnett children played, as their sisters had, in the hilly grounds of their family estate, making forts under the Torrey pines, eating mulberries and guavas and grapes, and – always – looking out for snakes. And, of course, they went to the beach.

Young Val on the beach, with the Del Mar pier in the background

Val and Coy Jr., 1933

But it wasn't all freedom and play for Val and Coy Junior. They also had school. Aunty Too tutored them at home, using the Calvert School Home Instruction Division, an early and long respected method of home-schooling. The lessons were challenging, but the children had a lot of loving help from Too.

Valentine would complete eighth grade by the time she was 12, a year when a lot would change in her life. With her brother already sent off to military academy, she would attend Marlborough, the private girls' school in Los Angeles where her sisters had gone. Val would dismiss the notion that there was anything special about starting high school at the age of 12, later saying of her homeschooling experience, "You learn fast when you're the only student."

Imagining Homeschooling

After our mother, Valentine, graduated from Marlborough at the age of 16 and went off to college, her old Calvert schoolbooks, including the engaging if largely inaccurate *A Child's History of the World*, were packed in boxes and stored upstairs in the shadowy, cavernous third-floor attic at my grandparents' house at 104 Fremont Place, near downtown Los Angeles, where they had moved during World War II, when they temporarily left Del Mar because of the war. In the 1950s, after opening presents and surviving Granddaddy Coy's speeches over Christmas dinner, we kids would sneak upstairs and play school with the old books. Since I was the oldest I usually got dibs on being the teacher. We were on vacation, but it was fun to play school, trying to imagine our mother's strange childhood as we used her books and pretended to be tutored at home.

Growing up as middle-class children in the 1950s, our life was solid and predictable. Playing school and pretending to be like Mama and her brother, we could not imagine the wild, frenetic glamour of life in the Twenties, nor the devastation that would come as it all collapsed.

Chapter 11

The Hoover Dam

As the 1930s dawned over the Tehachapi Mountains, the new decade had a different feeling than the last: Rather than promise, it held fear. Business was slow in those first years of the Great Depression, but the workers at the plant in the mountains pressed on. Monolith kept making cement, and the company, while holding its breath, was able to stay afloat.

While the vegetable gardens and small company profits kept things running at the Burnetts' place in Del Mar, costs had to be contained in those hard times. The long cherished plans – to move the original house from the top of the hill to another location on the property and replace it with the show-stopping Mediterranean-style mansion designed by Richard Requa – were sadly relinquished.

But all was not lost. Requa devised an addition to the wooden house, an entire two-story wing built of concrete, with bedrooms for the children and their nurses, and a second floor master suite and balcony with a glass partition to block the wind off the ocean while the parents sat and admired the view. Outside the original breakfast room, with its wide expanse of windows looking out over the rose garden, Requa designed a fountain inspired by his travels in Morocco and Spain. With the windows open in the morning, the family could hear the water splashing in the fountain and catch the scent of roses and a faint smell of the sea while they ate their soft-boiled eggs and drank freshly squeezed juice.

The remodeling provided an opportunity to showcase Monolith's latest product, colored cement. A patio of concrete in irregular shapes of varying colors was poured near the roses. The Craftsman-style house with the huge concrete addition and multicolored patio with the garden that seemed to have come straight from someplace on the Mediterranean was an incongruous mixture, but somehow it all worked.

The Requa-designed fountain outside the breakfast room at La Atalaya

Along with having a new product in its colored cement, in the early 1930s Monolith landed an important new contract, one that echoed the plant's earliest role – dealing with water. Long before the Los Angeles Aqueduct was built, there were hopes of finding a way to dam up and harness the water of the Colorado River. The debates about how and where to erect such a structure went on for years. In 1928, after much investigation, legislation and consternation, Congress authorized a new project, an unrivaled engineering challenge: the building of the Hoover Dam.

Such a project required years of planning and design before the actual building began. Leaders of several cement companies were consulted, including Coy Burnett, president of Monolith Portland Cement. Construction began in 1932, and Monolith ended up being one of the plants selected to supply the 335,000 barrels of cement ($428,800 worth) that went into the construction of the dam.

It was great to get the business, especially in those challenging times. But construction of the Hoover Dam also provided a unique opportunity – indeed, a demand – for any cement company involved, and that was to develop a better quality of cement than had ever been known. Building the Hoover Dam required cement so fine it could produce concrete with the strength and endurance to withstand time while retaining many tons of water – at full capacity exactly 26.12 million acre ft., or 32.22 cubic km.

If built using conventional methods, it would have taken 125 years for such an enormous amount of concrete to cool and dry. The massive dam required a different construction system. So a unique plan was developed, requiring special frames and coolants to create giant building blocks. Monolith and the other cement companies were on their A-game, making a finer grade of cement than ever before. The dam began to go up. Only time would tell.

When completed in 1936, the Hoover Dam was the largest project ever made with concrete. It was also the largest public works project in U. S. history. Three-and-a-quarter billion cubic yards of concrete went into its construction, with over a million more used in building the power plant and other works. The Lower Colorado Bureau of Reclamation estimates that there's enough concrete in the dam to pave a two-lane highway from San Francisco all the way to New York.

In terms of its holding power, concrete cores were removed from the dam for testing in 1995, and according to the American Society of Civil Engineers report, the dam's concrete had a compressive strength that far exceeded that of normal concrete. The study concluded that, nearly 60 years after its completion, "Hoover Dam's concrete has continued to slowly gain strength."

Coy would be so proud. Or maybe he'd just frown slightly and say, "Well, that's what you'd expect. Monolith cement."

Chapter 12

The Wall, Part One

However significant the Hoover Dam project was for Monolith's financial health, for the Burnetts there was an even more important function for Monolith cement during the early years of the Depression: its leading role in the construction of the wall.

The wall had been included in the overall design for La Atalaya from the very beginning, an "ornamental wall," as the early newspaper reports had described it, to set off the property and punctuate its Mediterranean villa flair. Concrete also had an important role in the gateways that were planned to open onto the different levels of the hilly property. Heavy concrete columns and gates of elaborate wrought iron grillwork were designed to welcome new arrivals with a flourish.

The economic crash in 1929 had put an end to the plans to build a Requa-designed mansion. But the wall was another thing.

As the hard times dug in, the divide between the haves and have-nots, which had grown deeper and wider during the Twenties, became a chasm. Bread-lines lengthened, as did the unemployment lines. Much of the nation faced poverty and heartbreak. All over the country angry stockholders, whose once promising shares were suddenly worthless, began rising up against company officials. Locking the doors of their fancy homes, executives tried to lie low.

As both president and principal owner of Monolith, Coy Burnett felt vulnerable and afraid for his family. The U. S. Census might have identified the property as a farm, but to almost anybody else it looked like an expensive estate, with all its buildings and gardens, clearly belonging to a man of means. Up there on the hill, for all to see, the Burnetts' property suddenly felt like a target.

So, in 1932, employing an unrecorded number of workmen and sacks of concrete, the wall finally got built. It surrounded the entire property, with three large gates giving access to the residence at the top; the garages, gardens and housing halfway down the hill; and the stables at the bottom. Above the main gate, which opened onto the drive at the top of the hill, Mexican tiles were placed in an arch, spelling out the estate's name, **LA ATALAYA**.

DEL MAR HISTORICAL SOCIETY

The main gate to La Atalaya, giving access through the wall to the residence. The tiles that arched over the gate spelled out "La Atalaya," Spanish for "The Lookout," or "The Watchtower." (This photo detail is reproduced from the book Del Mar Looking Back *by Nancy Hanks Ewing with permission from the publisher.)*

Throughout her life Valentine reminisced fondly about the family pets she loved as a girl, especially two big dogs by the names of Bruno and Buster, who would roughhouse and play fetch for hours. Remembering how isolated she was from other children, it's easy to imagine what the dogs meant to her, this chance to play, to throw sticks and balls and have them brought back by another living being.

But it's like King remembering the fancy dining room, not the record-breaking speed, of the SS *Bremen:* In Valentine's fondly shared childhood memories there was no hint of the real reason for the dogs. They were huge, muscular mastiffs, purchased for their size and intimidation potential, and allowed to roam freely on the multi-acre estate, a deterrent to anyone foolish enough to even think about climbing over the wall.

Mastiffs Bruno and Buster played double roles at La Atalaya: To the children, they were family pets, but they were acquired to patrol the property during the tense times of the Depression.

The gates were locked during those difficult days of the 1930s, the dogs were alert and the wall was ready for anything. Coy was reassured that he could keep his focus on the business.

Well, that and defending himself legally. The stockholders never scaled the wall at La Atalaya. Instead, they took Coy Burnett to court, the very year he built the wall, according to the *San Bernadino County Sun*:

Stockholders Seek To Recover Money

LOS ANGELES. Aug. 22, 1932. A group of stockholders in the Monolith Portland Cement Co. filed suit today agalnst Coy Burnett, president, and other executives, seeking to recover money which they claimed had been spent illegally and for personal pleasures. The plaintiffs also asked that title to 75,000 shares of company stock, valued at $1,150,000, which they said is held by the Monolith Corporation, be restored to the cement company. The complaint alleged that Burnett is virtually the owner of the Monolith Corporation.

The stockholders' claim sounds quite plausible. But as far as I know, throughout his long life and seemingly endless court battles, my grandfather Coy Burnett's self-assurance and legal acumen served him well, and he never lost a single legal contest.

Those challenges, along with keeping the business running, may have kept Coy distracted, but sitting in his rustic office across from the cement plant, isolated up in the Tehachapi Mountains, there's little doubt he yearned for the booming industry of the decade before. Ahh, for the days when he landed the deal with the City of Los Angeles and launched a thriving business, when he could afford to live in penthouse suites and take the family on exotic cruises and tours of Europe.

Coy was battling angry stockholders and the downward lunge of the Great Depression, but the 1930s did not quash his zeal for the grand gesture. Even as he secured the wall at La Atalaya and made sure his family was tucked away with their guard dogs behind locked gates, Coy was cooking up a new scheme.

One that involved the Pacific Ocean.

Chapter 13
Santa Catalina

Out in the ocean, 26 miles off the coast of what is now California, lies an archipelago, a group of islands, that has long been home to humans. About 7,000 years ago the People of the Earth, or *Tongva* in their language, were living on the mainland when a group of them took their *titi'at*, large canoes, and set out across the water to explore the islands. They liked what they saw and more Tongva joined them, settling in small villages all over one of the islands, which they called Pimu. There they enjoyed the abundant supply of native fish and game, and the soft soapstone which the Pimugnans carved into bowls and utensils to trade for skins, seeds and obsidian from the mainland.

There's a story that, many centuries later, descendants of these ancient Tongva paddled their canoes out to welcome Spanish explorers to the island. In truth, when Juan Rodríguez Cabrillo, leading the first European expedition to the area, arrived on the island in 1542, the Tongva resisted the invasion fiercely. Cabrillo himself was injured in the fighting and ultimately died. His expedition left the island, which Cabrillo had named San Salvador after his ship, without him, and the native people resumed their peaceful lives. But 60 years later another Spanish explorer "discovered" the island, on the eve of the Fiesta de Santa Catalina, inspiring a new name: Santa Catalina. Finding no valuable metals on the island, only what they noted as "more poor Indians," the Europeans left the island people alone again for another 150 years. But eventually the island was declared part of the Spanish Empire, and descendants of the original Pimugnans, those who had survived the hostility and diseases brought by the Europeans, were forced to leave and join fellow indigenous people on the mainland being "saved" by Christianity in the California missions.

The island had had numerous names and incarnations, but Santa Catalina – or just Catalina – stuck. With its excellent climate, secluded coves and proximity to the mainland, the island was a handy hideout for pirates from all over, who were joined through the years by fur traders, missionaries, smugglers and even the Union army. Numerous plans to develop its potential as a vacation spot finally took hold in the 20th century.

The early 20th century saw the island grow in popularity, and in the 1920s and '30s Catalina was again discovered, not by explorers this time but by movie stars and celebrities. Not surprisingly, given its proximity to the self-described movie capital of the world, the island became a popular destination for the Hollywood elite. Coy Burnett's name is among those listed as members of the private Tuna Club of Avalon in the Twenties, joining other anglers carrying on the traditions, and trying to beat the record, a 251-pound tuna landed by Colonel C. P. Morehouse back in 1899. So perhaps Coy was there into the Thirties as well, rubbing elbows with fellow members Charlie Chaplin and Stan Laurel. Or maybe Bing Crosby, who would later play an important role in the life of Del Mar.

The blue water, the fancy lodges, the glamorous tourists ... the whole scene at Catalina was a long way from the cement plant up in the Tehachapi Mountains and the multicultural families who lived and worked there. Maybe it was moving up to Monolith and living alongside the workers and their families that inspired Coy to start a new company tradition. Maybe it was nostalgia for those great ocean voyages with the family in the heyday of the Twenties. Maybe, in spite of his gruff manner and the difficulties he would later have relating to his grandchildren, Coy – the man with the endless supply of Clorets gum – had a soft spot for kids. Or maybe it was the way hard times can bring folks together.

Whatever the motivation, in the middle of the Great Depression Coy Burnett came up with an idea, and every summer from then until 1941, when World War II put an end to it, any child between the ages of 7 and 14 whose parent worked at the Monolith Portland Cement Company got to go on a trip. To Catalina Island, for a week, all expenses paid. Among the lucky kids who got to go were the children of the company president, Valentine Burnett and her siblings. For Valentine the Catalina trips were a highlight of her childhood. Being tutored at home, she didn't know many kids, so the summer adventure across the ocean to play with other children was a real treat.

The excited kids, and no less excited mothers who accompanied them, would board the Southern Pacific Special in Tehachapi and take it to the harbor in San Pedro, near Los Angeles, where they'd get on a boat and ride for a couple of hours across the ocean to the only city on Catalina, Avalon.

In the 1930s the little harbor city was a mix of glamour and rustic charm. Monolith set up its own tent city, wooden floors with canvas housing, like one big summer camp, sleeping hundreds. The company provided a cook, and there was a special cafeteria erected for the Monolith folks – the kids and 30 or more volunteer members of the Monolith Ladies Committee, chaperoning and enjoying their trip to the island every bit as much as their offspring. The diversity of the committee reflected that of the workforce: Rene Ramos, Faye Northwang, Eumatilda Warner, Isabel Cervantes, Nell Wilson, Carmen and Dolores Acedo.

In spite of living in California, for many of the children and some of their parents as well, this was the first time they had seen the ocean or been on a big boat. Even for Valentine, with her luxurious travel to Europe as an infant and her vacation paradise in Del Mar, those summer trips on the Monolith dime were exciting and exotic.

In July, 1938 *The Bakersfield Californian* ran a story about the Monolith company trips to Catalina, with a grainy photograph of the happy kids, "two hundred and five strong," running across the sand into the waves. "Tehachapi Youngsters on Annual Trip to Big Resort" reported that the group, including three children of the president, Coy Burnett, enjoyed everything "from double decker ice cream cones and popcorn to the glass-bottom boat, flying fish trip, and pony cart rides." The kids would never forget the starlight drives, weenie roasts, speedboat rides, canoeing, row boating, moonlight sings, volleyball and baseball games, fishing and trips to the Catalina Bird Park. On Catalina, everyone was just there to have fun, no matter whether the other kid's parent was an engineer, a laborer, a secretary or the president of the company.

There had been a mini gold rush on Catalina in the late 1800s, in spite of the fact that there was actually no confirmed sighting of gold there ever. Still, that didn't stop hopeful prospectors from making their way to the island. But even if they'd found lots of the precious metal, even if there had been mounds of gold nuggets, to the kids of Monolith and the moms who accompanied them, it could never have exceeded the value of those

The girls and women of what must have been one of the last of the Monolith Children's Weeks. Valentine Burnett is the tallest in the second row, in the dark sweater. The two young women in the middle of the back row are probably the older Burnett daughters, King and Anne, serving as chaperones.

glorious summer weeks during the Great Depression, living in a tent village on the sunny island of Santa Catalina.

Souvenir poster for the Monolith kids enjoying their week on Catalina Island in 1939. Activities shown include island tours, water sports, pony and cart rides, playing checkers, the Monolith parade through Avalon, and sack races, in which racers competed in Monolith Cement sacks (bottom row, second from left).

Chapter 14

The Lookout

The Catalina trips, with their merriment and play, were a high point of the 1930s, but they were the exception. Still, hard times have one important thing in common with good times: They don't last forever. The Great Depression wound down as people began to get alarmed about other things, particularly the rise of fascism and the increasing prominence of a man named Adolph Hitler. Another world war began to look inevitable. With the threat of Japan's increasing mobilization just across the Pacific, the village of Del Mar, which had been a bit sleepy during the hard years of the 1930s, woke up.

Southern California's position on the west coast of the United States was considered strategic. And vulnerable. Up and down the coast of the United States, preparations were being made for war.

Activity was especially apparent near Del Mar. After all, the city of San Diego, just a few miles to the south, was an important headquarters of the Pacific Fleet, having long been a big "Navy town." Even before Pearl Harbor, in November of 1940 a large army encampment was built just four miles south of Del Mar. Set among the Torrey pines along the shore, the camp was established for training coast artillerymen and anti-aircraft gunners.

After Pearl Harbor, things got lively indeed in little Del Mar. The Naval Auxiliary Air Facility took over the small air strip in the flat river valley to the east and below the hilltop where La Atalaya perched. It was intended to be a landing field for small aircraft but it had a short runway, so it became a base for blimps used in anti-submarine reconnaissance.

A training facility was set up at the Del Mar Fairgrounds, with temporary barracks, galleys, mess halls, offices, recreational facilities and classrooms for those stationed at the airfield. The fairgrounds was also the site of manufacturing tail assemblies for the B-17 bomber being built by Douglas Aircraft, located in Long Beach. Near the fairgrounds, at the racetrack, paratroopers slept in stalls usually reserved for Thoroughbreds. By 1942, Marines from Camp Pendleton, a few miles to the north of town, ran and trained for amphibious warfare on the Del Mar beaches. Even The Plunge was taken over by the military, and soldiers and sailors had to prove they could swim by jumping off the 1,000-foot pier.

The Del Mar hill, with its tall leafy eucalyptus trees and rocky ledges, provided excellent cover for anti-aircraft batteries, and sandbagged observation posts were dug into the western side of the ridge, facing out over the Pacific and potential invasion.

Still, as lookout locations went, there was one clearly superior site in Del Mar, on the northern end of the ridge at the very top of the hill. It's easy to imagine a group of military officials exploring the area and thinking at the time how the place was perfectly located, like it had always been meant to be used as some kind of watch station. And if someone among them understood Spanish, they might have pointed, saying, "The funny thing is, that's its name, right there on the big gate into the property: 'La Atalaya.' The Lookout!"

But before all that, with the rumblings of war growing louder, Coy and Mildred were nervous about Del Mar's potentially dangerous location near prime military installations. They decided to move their family back to Los Angeles. Monolith was doing well again, thanks to the Hoover Dam and several municipal projects, and Coy could afford to relocate the entire family and primary staff. So in 1940 they left Del Mar and La Atalaya for downtown L. A. They settled into Apartment Z, the penthouse suite, at the Biltmore Hotel. It was an uneasy peace.

Pearl Harbor changed everything. Valentine, almost 13, quickly learned never to turn on a lamp before proper care was taken. At sunset she watched as the hotel staff carefully pulled the usual drapes, and then the heavy blackout curtains over every window, muffling the city noises below, the sounds that were so different from those in Del Mar. There were no crickets chirping from the slough. Instead of the songs of birds calling and the wind in the trees, she heard the steady drone of traffic, sirens, angry horns blasting faintly below. Then, as it grew dark, it became silent in an unnatural way.

It wasn't the pulling of the blackout curtains that Val would remember most vividly from that time, but the family's other nighttime ritual. After getting ready for bed, with her robe over her pajamas, she would slide on her slippers, grab her toothbrush and, along with the rest of the family and live-in staff, she'd ride the elevator down several floors, to Apt. J, halfway between Apt. Z on the top floor and the lobby on the first floor. It was there that the family slept for the night. Coy, concerned about the potential for nighttime bombings, judged the penthouse too hazardous a place to sleep. However, concern about gas warfare was high during WWII, and he figured the lower floors also posed risks. As with most challenges, he believed he had a solution. In this case it was a rare compromise: Strike a balance and rent a second set of rooms, right in the middle of the hotel. Falling bombs and deadly gases be damned.

So Valentine didn't spend those war years in Del Mar watching tactical maneuvers on the beach or gazing to the east as tethered blimps bobbed over the airstrip, a little comical in spite of their sober purpose. With the military getting ready to commandeer their house and property for the war effort, the family had packed up all their belongings. They had brought some of the most valuable with them to Los Angeles, but they stored most of their things at La Atalaya. The furniture was pushed against the walls, next to the grand piano, and covered with dustsheets. The dishes and books, photographs and records were packed up in boxes and set carefully in the spare rooms, to wait the hopefully short time until the war was over and everything could get back to normal.

And although there is no record whatsoever of any enemy fire or suspicious activity in Del Mar during the Second World War, no one could have known that would be the case during those scary days, awaiting worldwide war. It might be coming across the ocean, and a watchful La Atalaya stood tall and fearless, ready to do her job and proud to be of service.

Chapter 15

104 Fremont Place

One morning after the attack on Pearl Harbor, Mildred and Coy were having breakfast in their suite at the Biltmore when something caught their eye in the classified section of the *Los Angeles Times*. It was a large advertisement offering for sale an "unusual 18th-century French chateau" in an exclusive gated community right off Wilshire Boulevard. The address was 104 Fremont Place.

The house was not, of course, from the 18th century, since that would mean it was constructed alongside the primitive missions being built as part of Father Serra's colonizing efforts. But while the house was not actually that old, it certainly was a chateau.

Fremont Place had been conceived about 30 years earlier, advertised at the time without fear of appearing hyperbolic: "The most exclusive and highest class residence community in the most desirable residential city

DUNCAN MAGINNIS, HISTORICLOSANGELES.ORG

The "18th-century French chateau" at 104 Fremont Place in Los Angeles

in America – Fremont Place. There is no other residence property in Los Angeles to compare with it – no property which gives the man of means such opportunity for exclusiveness – such unique home attractions."

At first the men of means were slow to arrive, but gradually people bought into the idea of living in the exclusive neighborhood with the impressive gates and large lots, tucked away and secluded but close to downtown L. A. During the Twenties and into the Thirties the houses began to rise and Fremont Place started to resemble a fantasy land, its villas and chateaus and manor houses seemingly plucked from various countries and different eras, all brought together in one beautiful setting, off Wilshire Boulevard.

Two people drawn to building their dream mansion on the winding streets of Fremont Place were Florence and Charles Wild, from Milwaukee. They purchased their exclusive lot at #104 and commissioned architect Elmer Gray, who designed for them a house fit for wealthy landowners in 18th-century France, with four master suites, extensive public rooms and servants' quarters, and a grand foyer with a magnificent sweeping staircase and a wall of French doors opening onto a flagstone patio and the enclosed backyard. But the Wilds were not able to settle in peacefully. After nearly 10 years and lots of family drama, they put their chateau on the market. And eventually sold it, in 1942, to Coy and Mildred Burnett.

In spite of the war, Coy apparently decided that having his own place was worth the risk of being bombed or gassed to death. So Valentine and her family moved out of the penthouse at the Biltmore and into the house at 104 Fremont Place. Jessie and Houston came too of course, and the cook and others. There was a whole wing of the house, as well a place over the multicar garage, for the staff. And so, in spite of his role in establishing the look of Southern California architecture, Coy Burnett spent the last 30 years of his life not in a Mediterranean-style villa, but in a French-style chateau.

Living at the country club or in hotels had given Mildred complete freedom from the rigors of housekeeping. Then they bought the house in Fremont Place.

The chateau had to be properly outfitted, but Mildred was no homemaker. So she turned to the Gorham Silver Company catalogue, selecting a pattern called Etruscan. She then ordered a dozen of everything, with a stylized "B" engraved on each piece. Not just place settings. There were a dozen individual sterling silver coffee carafes and individual tea pots, a dozen mint juleps, a dozen silver champagne saucers lined with gold wash so the silver wouldn't spoil the taste of the bubbly.

One of the Burnetts' Gorham Etruscan silver coffee servers, monogrammed "B"

Mementos

When my grandparents died, Mama made sure to get a few of the old sterling pieces for her children to have as keepsakes. Like her exquisite silk baby clothes from Paris or the bits of broken, charred china we kids found buried around the ruins at La Atalaya, the silver goblets with the gold wash tell my grandparents' story in ways words cannot.

In the early years of the war, Kingsbury was a single woman in her mid twenties, living at home in Fremont Place. Hoping to contribute to the war effort, she initially joined the Red Cross, working in a blood bank and making bandages and packing supplies for the troops, but she found she was disappointed by the lack of camaraderie at the Red Cross.

So she enlisted, in the Marines. Since it was inconceivable, in those days, for a woman to be involved in combat, King was stationed stateside, but on the east coast, far away from family. Her duties included driving military vehicles, which no doubt pleased her since she had always enjoyed driving. Coy wrote to his eldest child every week during that time, the only personal record left in his own words. Typed, they were no doubt dictated to his secretary, yet the words reveal Coy's respect for his daughter, his desire to reassure her as her father, and an unexpected tenderness.

Miss Kingsbury M. Burnett

November 10, 1943

Dear King:

Herewith enclosed please find the bank statement of your account.

Business is going rather uncertainly, and it is a question whether we will make any money over-all this year in the cement business. However, we have made money twenty-one out of twenty-three years and we can probably stand it to not make any money this year and next, or so long as the war is on.

[The letter goes on for several paragraphs, in detailed discussion about football, specifically how the USC Trojans were doing. Not only were Coy and Mildred big Trojan fans, but it was also King's alma mater.]

I have been reading your letters with interest, and while I am not able to follow your logic in refusing advancement, still I am glad to assume that you have analyzed the situation carefully and have made the right decision.

We are all looking forward with interest to your progress and the various moves you make, and know that you will keep us posted.

With much love, I am

Daddy

Valentine was 14 years old when her sister King joined the Marines, and her correspondence with her sister during that time was full of news about school, friends, the latest movies and going to the ballet. But she was also at home, observing and reporting from behind the scenes. Her letter, postmarked the same day as her father's, sheds light on Coy's struggle to strike such a supportive tone with his eldest daughter's decisions:

Tuesday

Dear King,

If you have rec'd mother's letter I suppose you know that everyone thinks you're crazy for refusing officer's training or whatever it is. Except me. I'd rather drive a truck, too. Papa's a little irked. You've gotten in something he can't mess with. Congratulations!

Keeping the Monolith plant running and serving in the military weren't the only efforts being made by the Burnett family. Everyone pitched in during those war years. In her own letter to King, dated October 1943, Mildred wrote, "I think I told you that Bud was building some shelves in the basement, and Too and I have arranged all of our 700 quarts of fruit pickles, chili sauce, catsup and juice . . . along with all of the other canned goods, jams, jellies and preserves." It wasn't without duress for Mildred, all this involvement in her kitchen. Later in the letter she admitted, "I still don't enjoy this planning and buying of food. But I find that I am not the only one doing it, and I meet someone I know nearly every time I go out. Women from Town and Gown, mothers from Black-Foxe Academy and Marlborough . . ." She was consoled, apparently, knowing she wasn't the only woman of means who suddenly found herself in the kitchen.

The most exciting thing that ever happened at 104 Fremont Place was the wedding, in the summer of 1948, of the couple who, two years later, would become my parents. Valentine Burnett was married to the handsome young man she had met in school at Berkeley, Lloyd Rentsch. The grand occasion afforded her parents, never much for socializing, the chance to repay all their societal obligations, and literally hundreds of people gathered in the gardens to watch the young bride and groom exchange their vows and, with big smiles, slice into the towering wedding cake.

Valentine Burnett and Lloyd Rentsch were married in the gardens at 104 Fremont Place.

A band played, the champagne flowed and people danced into the night, while Coy smoked cigars and held court with his cronies in the Smoking Room. The next morning, the front page of the society section was dominated by a photograph of the event, the young couple with their dazzling smiles as they walked down the beribboned garden path, looking like minor royalty, or at least Hollywood movie stars.

Christmas Dinners at 104

While every August of my childhood meant walking the wall and endless days on the beach at Del Mar, every Christmas until I left for college held another family ritual. After opening our presents at home, we would all dress up, pile into the latest station wagon, and leaving empty stockings and mountains of torn wrappings and ribbon behind, we'd drive an hour from our home in Rolling Hills into Los Angeles proper, to Fremont Place, for holiday dinner with the family.

A towering Christmas tree always filled one corner of Grandmother and Granddaddy's huge living room, right by the grand piano. The dining room held two massive sideboards, decorated for the holidays and laden with food. The dining table sat in the middle, expanded into a giant square.

The room was lovely, but that didn't make up for us kids being held hostage, over our dessert plates, while Granddaddy made a long speech about "the Company." In our family, and particularly around my grandfather, the Monolith Portland Cement Company was never far away. Befitting its name, Monolith loomed large in our family's life, more like a deity than a simple cement plant or mere company.

So it was not unusual to find managers from Monolith at the big table, joining in the festivities with family members. As kids we were relieved when too many adults came to share Christmas dinner, because that meant we were allowed to eat in the breakfast room. That space, a multi-sided room with recessed shelves that held French china and in the center a six-sided wrought iron table topped with glass, held no resemblance to the dark formal dining room from which we had mercifully been banished.

A perfect breakfast room, it was light and airy. Multiple French doors opened out to the backyard with its towering old evergreens festooned in moss and its fountain filled with old koi.

After the meal we'd slip outside, playing among the big trees and trying to glimpse the big fish through the lily pads and algae in the fountain. The backyard was shaded under a canopy of trees, its fetid smell cut by the sharp tang of evergreens, its stillness interrupted by the splashing of water. Of course, there was a gardener, maybe more than one, who cared for the grounds, but for us kids it was a secret place where only children ventured, magically removed from the city around it.

Sometimes we couldn't escape out back, and my mother was fond of a story about such a time. I was sitting at the grown-up table, next to Mama, 5 or 6 years old, all dressed up and stuck listening to my grandfather as he droned on about "the Company" and who was in or out of favor with him at that particular moment. As he wound down, according to my mother, I turned to her with great concern and whispered, "Why does Granddaddy have so many enemies?" No matter how many times she told that story, my mother always seemed freshly humored by it.

My grandparents' "18th-century chateau" boasted quite a collection of modern conveniences. The kitchen had a walk-in refrigerator and, on the second floor, set into a wall, were doors that opened to reveal a heated "sweat closet." There my health-conscious grandparents lay prone and perspired away their impurities.

Off the grand foyer, across from Granddaddy's study, was the elevator my grandparents had installed for Aunty Too, when cancer of the jaw left her too weak to walk upstairs. We kids only knew our great aunt, the woman who had tutored our mother, as an invalid. Often bedridden in an upstairs bedroom at 104 Fremont Place, she always held a tissue to her mouth, to catch the saliva she could not contain after having parts of her tongue and jaw removed. We kids just accepted it, tissue and all. We liked riding up and down in the elevator, and we liked hanging out with Aunty Too. Patrick and Tim did especially, because Too had a hospital bed she let them operate, and one of the heavy metal boxes for remote controlling the television. Watching TV and mumbling through her drooling was about all Aunty Too could do during those years, but she was a former school teacher and seemed to brighten during our visits. Although he was quite little, Pat could understand her when she spoke, while most people couldn't.

In addition to the elevator for Aunty Too, a motorized chair was installed on tracks that ran up the back stairs, giving her two ways to get upstairs and down. The chair was good for Houston also, after his legs were amputated. When we kids were allowed to play on it, we'd ride up and down the stairs, like a carnival ride.

It might have looked like it was plucked from an estate outside Paris, but the elegant French chateau–style house at 104 came equipped with so many modern devices it seemed more the House of the Future at Disneyland than the home of ordinary people.

But were Coy and Mildred Burnett ordinary folks? Going from rural Nebraska to owning a walled estate and one of the mansions of Los Angeles is a long leap. It may explain some of Coy's success. Maybe his drive to succeed masked a secret fear that he was an outsider, an imposter. Mildred, so private and remote, may have felt that way too. She certainly disdained the usual conventions unless they were necessary, and clearly did not share the interests of the typical housewife of her era. When they had purchased the house in Del Mar, it had come fully furnished, with the former owners' pots and pans, china and pottery, none of which she ever replaced. She was glad to avoid the responsibility, maybe, or she just didn't care about those things.

Mansions of Los Angeles

A quarter of a century after my grandparents first saw the ad for 104 Fremont in the *L. A. Times*, I was sitting at the orthodontist's office, waiting for the next "adjustment" to the torture devices inside my mouth. Trying to distract myself, I looked around for something to read. No to *Highlights*. Ditto *Time* magazine. The newspaper looked good until I realized somebody had stolen the funnies. Desperate, I dug to the bottom of the pile and found a slim hardbound book with photographs and a gold stamped title: *Mansions of Los Angeles*. I began to leaf through it, idly, with little faith in its value to distract me from the dread of what awaited me in the orthodontist's chair.

Then, halfway through my page-flipping, something caught my eye and made me forget my anxiety momentarily.

I stared at the photo of the lovely 18th-century-French-style house with the circular driveway, the pots of topiary flanking the portico, and two curlicue "B's" worked into the fancy wrought iron work on the elegant front doors. "B" for Burnett. It wasn't my imagination. There in the mansions book - it was my grandparents' house! I checked the small print identifying the location. Yup. 104 Fremont Place.

The 2011 Oscars for Best Picture, Best Director and Best Actor all went to a French film called *The Artist*. It's a movie about the early movie industry and a Douglas Fairbanks–type actor, Georges Valentin, set in the exciting world of 1920s Los Angeles. *The Artist* is remarkable, not only for being filmed in black-and-white, or even for its excellence, but because it is almost entirely silent. As the film begins, Georges is living in a French chateau–style house with a grand front entrance with ornate wrought iron doors. When the wide double doors are opened, there appears a letter – complete with curlicues – clearly visible on each side, worked into the beautifully crafted wrought iron. The letter "B."

It may not have had the allure of La Atalaya, with her acreage and her view, but the property at 104 Fremont Place was a star in its own right. From serving as the setting of a real-life post-war society wedding, then being featured in a book alongside other early mansions of Los Angeles, to providing the elegant "residence" of an imaginary movie star in an award-winning film, my grandparents' Los Angeles home for more than 30 years got to play some pretty glamorous roles.

Chapter 16

FIRE!

There are many stories about that sad time early in World War II when the fancy house at La Atalaya – the Arts and Crafts cottage originally owned by Caroline Schafer and then embellished by Richard Requa, the home where Coy found sanctuary from the hustle bustle of the city and where Valentine spent her childhood – went up in smoke.

There was abundant unfounded speculation about how the fire started, and there remains some confusion still about exactly when it happened. Some blamed the military. Rumors flew, alleging carelessness on the part of military personnel who may or may not have been guarding the observation post. Others claimed the fire happened at night, that people unknown had sneaked in and were partying there. Folks seeking further drama insisted it was a wild bash on New Year's Eve. The most paranoid asserted that it was arson.

The fire marshal told Coy and Mildred that the fire was caused by an electrical short and that, fortunately, no one was there when it happened. He said the fire was so hot it melted metal.

Fire is a ruthless force, and it was ruthless indeed when it visited La Atalaya. With no apology whatsoever, it gobbled up the carefully folded drapes and Oriental rugs in one enormous hot gulp, leaping onto the upholstered chairs and grand piano that stood pushed into a corner of the living room. The flames raced through the original wooden house and into the spacious Requa addition, indiscriminate, taking everything in their path.

The fire didn't care what it meant to the family when it came to the rooms storing their favorite books and precious mementos, the thick records played at 78 rpm, the record player that provided so much entertainment.

And when it came upon the boxes of family photos, many of them taken by quiet, observant Mildred, the chemicals and paper must have made the flames leap high, bright yellow and orange. The fire must have cackled joyfully, as if gloating.

The day it happened, we're told, the smoke could be seen from the Tudor-style buildings in downtown Del Mar. It could be seen by the school kids, walking home after class, who would later tell stories about it to their grandkids. And it could be seen from the Fairgrounds below the ridge, where the California Division of Forestry had built a fire station a few years before.

The firefighters jumped into their truck and drove as fast as the winding roads would let them, up to the top of the hill, where La Atalaya stood burning. They made it in time, and they thought they could save the house, or at least stop the fire from taking everything.

But it turned out they didn't have enough water, up there at the top of the hill. They couldn't get the pressure to power the fire hoses to do their job. The firefighters were left standing in the garden, next to the patio with its multicolored pavers, the big hoses hanging limp in their hands.

They watched helplessly as the once lovely home turned into a monument of brilliant flame and scorching heat, and then became a ruin.

Chapter 17

From the Ashes

The fire that destroyed my mother Valentine's childhood home became family lore, a dark smoky shadow woven into our ancestral history. It carried such mythic importance that it was easy to forget that it happened less than a decade before I was born in 1950. Never rebuilt, the ruins at the top of the hill made La Atalaya seem like an historic, even ancient, place.

It became a family ritual, going to see the ruins. At some point every August during the 1950s and '60s we kids would jam our protesting feet, so used to the freedom of being bare, into tennis shoes. We did this willingly, but, other than the day we got to go to the racetrack with our grandparents, it was the only time we wore shoes all month.

It was a steep climb from where we stayed in the remodeled garage at the midlevel of the estate up the overgrown switchback path winding among the trees and brush all the way to the top of the hill. Somebody carried a long stick, in case of rattlesnakes, but we rarely encountered anything other than lizards – unmoving, their eyes watching steadily as we approached, until suddenly, in a flash, they darted into the brush. Snakes weren't the only menace on that path, though. Sand burrs, those long grasses filled with prickly seed casings that make it on almost every state's "noxious weed" list, were everywhere. Slithering along the sandy trail or out from under rocks, the burrs grabbed onto our socks and shoes. Or our flesh, if we weren't so lucky. Nearly impossible to get out without an additional prick or two.

At the top of the path we'd find a clearing, the old concrete collapsed into the tangled grasses. Each visit we'd poke among the weeds till we found traces of the fountain, the rubble of old walls marking its contours. When we were little, the red brick chimney was still standing, two stories tall and proudly refusing to come down, as if proclaiming it once was part of a lovely residence. We knew we had to stay clear of that chimney, which could fall any minute, and we were never to go down into the deep dugout basement, where lizards ran around a huge old stove that lay charred and rusting where it had landed on its side. Sometime in the early '60s somebody knocked the chimney down, probably to prevent it from falling accidentally.

Being children, with no experience of what was once there, we had no real sense of the loss the ruins represented. For us they were a source of intrigue and excitement, including the thrill of possible danger with the chimney that might topple down on our heads. We knew our mother's family didn't get hurt, because they had already moved up to L. A. when the fire happened. To us it was just an interesting story, one of many about our mother's strange childhood. Being kids, we were happily self-centered: It was now, and we got to go to Del Mar, and that's what mattered.

Our final stop before heading back down the hill was the main gate where LA ATALAYA was spelled out in tiles, the wrought-iron gates padlocked heavily. In the clearing stood a concrete block with a step built into it. It showed no signs of fire. We knew that in earlier times the gate would have been wide open, and that where we stood would have been the circular driveway, with the concrete step used for mounting horses, ridden up from the stables at the bottom of the property.

Standing on that mounting block and looking back and forth between the ruins and the grand arching gate, we tried to imagine what it was like for our mother, a young teenager at the time, when her childhood home and everything in it completely disappeared.

Then we'd head back down the hill, to the place we knew as our summer home. Sometime between the end of World War II and the early 1950s, when I have my own first memories of going to Del Mar, my grandparents' property, the glamorous-estate-turned-working-farm-turned-wartime-lookout-turned-charred-ruins, transformed once again. One thing you can say about La Atalaya: She's never been afraid of change.

After the fire it had been clear that if the family was going to be able to return and use the property, some form of residence had to be reclaimed or built anew. The site at the top of the hill, with its picturesque pines amongst stony outcroppings and its panoramic view of the sea, was abandoned to the ashes and melted metal and broken crockery. There it would lie undisturbed for over 60 years, a memorial to my mother's life before the war.

Instead of that hilltop vista, the area chosen for the rebuild was the level stretch partway down the eastern slope of the property, where the greenhouses and garages, chicken coops and other buildings were located. The largest structure, with multiple garage stalls on the ground level and living quarters for the chauffeur and handymen above, was chosen, and transformed into a vacation home. It was there that we – my siblings and cousins and I – stockpiled almost two decades' worth of carefree memories.

Of course, all the buildings on that level of my grandparents' property were designed by Richard Requa in the mid-1920s, with red-tile roofs and his signature Mediterranean flair on the exterior. It wasn't all flimsy glamour back then. That garage was built to last – possibly it would have survived a nuclear attack. As others would later discover when they tried to renovate the building, there was only so much remodeling that could be done. So each garage stall was turned into a bedroom, just big enough for a dresser, ladder and chunky wooden bunkbed, with the garage doors walled over, and the front wall equipped with a series of regular doors through to the outside. The kitchen and living area were accessible on the left side of the building and, right in the middle, there was an outer door that opened onto a staircase leading upstairs, where the adults in the family slept. The stairs to the second floor were made of poured concrete, as were the walls on each side as the stairs. This made the stairwell exceptional for a couple of reasons. First, the acoustics. As a young teenager I discovered that if I sat on the top step and sang, my voice would reverberate as it was amplified by bouncing between the concrete surfaces. On days we weren't at the beach, when my grandparents and the other adults were at the races, I'd climb the stairs, sit on the top step and sing.

Not only was it perfect for its acoustics, but the concrete stairwell was also a cool spot on hot summer afternoons, and as such it attracted other visitors besides me. On at least two occasions a scream had us all running from our play outside to the door that led to the second floor, where we found the screamer pointing frantically – at a scorpion, inching its way up the stairs. The scorpion's stinger pulsed, daring anyone to come closer. Somebody went to get a shovel, and, amidst great excitement, the poisonous intruder was removed.

I don't know what the phoenix looked like as it rose from the legendary ashes and made its way again, anew, but I imagine it appeared a bit rough. Resurrection requires sturdy resilience, not beauty. Richard Requa's original design, with the red tile roof and outside terrace off the second floor, continued to give the building a Mediterranean feel. But with its long concrete profile and the multiple doors opening onto a vast paved driveway, our turquoise-blue-and-white station wagon and maybe one of Granddaddy's limos parked right in front, our family's summertime home in Del Mar did call to mind a comfortable though slightly run-down mid-century motel, maybe along Route 66.

But it was *our* motel, and – at least in our eyes – it was heaven.

Arriving at "our motel" with the station wagon and the family pets. In the front row (left to right) are Claire, Patrick, Tim, Jessie and me.

Chapter 18

The Wall, Part Two

While the residence at our family's place in Del Mar was somewhat funky, the wall surrounding it was something altogether different. For my generation it was like the wall had been there always, growing up out of the sandy soil like a very long shoot of concrete ivy. It seemed to have roots securing it as it climbed up and down the steep hillside, winding its way among the brush and iceplant, the eucalyptus and Torrey pines. Encircling, embracing the acres within, the wall was intrinsic to our sense of place, of family.

The wall's creation had been quite a feat. Large tall molds were constructed and the concrete (I need hardly say, made with Monolith cement) was poured into them, sinking deep into the soil. The concrete was so heavy it seemed to fuse with the earth and, as it hardened, become one with the hilly slope and stony outcroppings. The wall was a foot thick, definitely built to last, and the workers erected wider square columns every 10 feet or so, making it even more secure, and later giving us kids a wider place to rest and catch our breath before moving on to the next stretch of wall-walking.

A gate was built at the bottom of the property. When we came there in the 1950s it was rusted shut, surrounded by weeds. There were sand-burrs everywhere. The burrs and the thorny "itch weed" competed with the snakes to see who could make that part of the property the least appealing. But that didn't really matter, at least to our generation, because we never went down there, except when we were just moving through, atop the wall. No one went down there anymore. Still, we knew that in Mama's childhood there were gardens and horse stables down there.

Midway up the property was a large wrought-iron gate that in Mama's day led to the garages and outbuildings, gardens and staff's quarters.

But after the fire it became the main access to the property, opening onto the long wide driveway that sloped gently downward into the wide paved area in front of what became the somewhat motellike residence. It was the only gate I ever saw open.

The original main gate had been erected at the very top of the hill. Until the fire this gate gave access to the original home from Serpentine Drive, the perfect name for a street that winds up to the gate, curls around and then slides back down the hill.

Valentine's older sister Kingsbury riding at La Atalaya, with the stables behind her and the mid-level buildings up the hill

There are many stories about the wall, just as there are about my grandparents' property and Del Mar itself, their fortunes each having some steep ups and downs. Probably the best known legend about the wall, and the one that drove our family crazy, was the one about my mother.

That story was meant to explain the name "the Snake Wall." But the name itself was fiction. At some point somebody called the protective, ornamental wall that enclosed the La Atalaya estate the "Snake Wall," and people came to refer to the estate itself as "the Snakewall property." Maybe the name was just too good to resist, with the main gate off Serpentine Drive, and the wall, like the drive itself, resembling an enormous snake as it slithered and wound up and down the hilly property.

But just saying the wall looked snakelike lacked the drama and pull of a good story. The lore about the wall and my mother had more intrigue. According to legend, little baby Valentine was so deathly afraid of snakes that her doting, chivalrous father had an enormous wall built, to keep his precious darling safe.

My mother laughed it off, quick to point out that the facts didn't even line up. After all, the plan to build the wall was documented as early as 1925, in the *Coast Dispatch*, and she wasn't even born until 1929. She found particularly amusing the image of little Valentine's ambitious, driven father being so consumed with worry and fuss about his youngest child that he would have a wall built.

Mama Was Never Afraid of Snakes

However the name "Snake Wall" came about, the story about our mother's fear of snakes was pretty funny. For one thing, it was our dad, not mom, who was afraid, a fact we'd discovered one Saturday afternoon when we were watching the matinee of the *Million Dollar Movie* on Channel 9. It was just us four kids and Papa, snuggled up on the two loveseats in the den at our house in Rolling Hills. This was a rare treat, as he was usually traveling all week for work and often busy weekends, too. We were all glued to the black-and-white screen. Tarzan and Jane were moving cautiously through the jungle, trying to get away from the bad guys, when a giant serpent suddenly swung down from the low-hanging branches of a tree. Papa gasped, jumping involuntarily in his seat as we muffled our giggles.

Mama was never afraid of snakes, and somewhere there's a photo to prove it. She was volunteering on the L. A. Zoo Mobile the day the picture was taken, smiling and holding a very large serpent as it coiled up her arm and over her shoulders. I think she liked that picture partly because it set the record straight: She had no problem when it came to snakes. But she understood my father's fearful reaction, explaining to us kids that we humans, as primates, have an innate fear of snakes because they are a natural threat to us.

Valentine Burnett Rentsch and friend, in a photo takn during travels in Indonesia

The most amusing aspect of the folklore about Mama and the "protection" of the Snake Wall was the fact that the wall, while it kept some snakes out, also kept plenty of snakes inside the property. With the people. This was a problem, because these weren't just snakes, they were rattlesnakes.

When it came to rattlers, we knew we should be afraid. This fear was instilled in us as kids, through instructions that were drilled into us about how to handle snakebite. Although it would later be debunked, back then we thought we knew the right thing to do if someone got bitten by a rattlesnake. The treatment was to take a sharp knife and cut a fairly deep slice into the bite, then suck on it and spit out the poison (and the blood). Privately I doubted I could ever pull this off, even if I did just happen to have a knife handy, and even though I had excellent motivation, in the form of a chilling story about someone we knew.

He was the son of the couple who were caretakers of La Atalaya when our family wasn't there, which is when he was attacked by a rattler. By the time they got help he had to have his entire arm cut open, in a spiral, around and around from fingers to wrist to shoulder, in order to drain the poison. He had to have hundreds of stitches that left winding scars that fascinated and horrified us kids when we saw him the following August. They said he was "lucky" because the poison hadn't gone to his heart. Later he claimed the Snake Wall was actually named for him. The legend grew.

The rattlesnakes on the property and the threat they posed were a real problem. But unlike some problems, this one had a solution. An exciting solution, at least for us kids.

We were playing with the hose, spraying down the wide expanse of concrete driveway, watering the few flowers and more often each other. The four of us Rentsch kids – me, Tim, Claire and Pat – were in full summer mode: skin browned and hair lightened and a little salty from our days at the beach, a minimum of clothing, barefoot like me or maybe wearing rubber flip-flops, which back then we called thongs. The driveway was rough under my feet, and the cold water from the hose made chilly little puddles on the hot concrete. I was walking barefoot across them, hot, cool, hot, cool, when a white van came through the gates. We watched, curious, as it came slowly down the driveway. We didn't get many visitors.

The van stopped near the wire mesh fence that was supposed to keep the rattlers on the untamed side of the property, out of the yard. There was a clump of wild amaryllis just on the other side of the fence, and the lipstick-pink flowers on tall straight stalks looked like flags. The sweet spicy perfume of the flowers intermingled with the steamy smell of the wet pavement as we gathered around the vehicle.

A man got out of the van and walked to the back, and we followed. Unlocking the doors, he slowly took out a large crate, then two more, and set them on the driveway. We got a little closer. Opening one of the crates, he carefully extracted a very large snake. We all stepped back.

"What kind of snake is that?" As usual, our little brother Patrick asked the question on all our minds.

"King snake."

"Does it bite?"

"Not us. King snakes are harmless to humans. Want to hold it?"

Pause.

Then, nonchalantly, "Sure."

The man solemnly handed one snake to each of us four slightly breathless kids. We could feel the cold, muscular bodies trying to slither up our arms. Getting bolder, we held their heads up and looked closely at their bright knowing little eyes and their flickering tongues.

We finally had to give them back to the man, who then walked over to the wire mesh fence. He made a little show for us as he released the king snakes, one at a time, onto the other side of the fence. We watched as they disappeared, slipping into the dry brush where they would make a new home and seek out their favorite foods, among them rattlesnake.

We resumed our usual play, knowing even then it was a memorable day.

As far as the snakes at La Atalaya, it was actually our grandmother who was afraid of them. The story was that in 1927 or so, Mildred insisted on moving the family from Del Mar back to Los Angeles for a while after a rattlesnake was spotted on the property, a year or two before my mother's birth. Maybe her aversion to snakes was one of the reasons that Grandmother often stayed with my grandfather in the city during those years, living in a hotel or the country club while the rest of the family stayed at Del Mar.

The facts did not hinder the retelling of the stories about Valentine and her fear of snakes and her doting daddy and why the wall was built. Somehow our family estate's beautiful name morphed with this imaginary tale, and, from formal minutes of the Del Mar City Council meetings to articles in the *Los Angeles Times* to books at the Del Mar Historical Society, La Atalaya became commonly referred to as the "Snakewall Property."

Chapter 19
Jessie

Growing up, I don't remember a summer without Del Mar. And I don't remember life without Jessie. No story about La Atalaya, or my family's history, would be complete if it didn't include her. Loving, warm, playful, faithful, intriguing, Jessie had many good qualities, and once you'd had her fried chicken you were ruined for anyone else's. But above all else, Jessie was lovingly there. Safe. Reliable. And reassuringly predictable.

Take, for example, her turns of phrase. Jessie had sayings for every occasion, and she used them devotedly. "Tomorrow-God-willing" was a phrase I heard so consistently as a child I thought "tomorrow" was an abbreviation.

When we kids acted up, Jessie would shake her head in disapproval, her deep "MMNH, MMNH, MMNH!" a clear indication that we were pushing the limits of even her abundant patience. Sometimes we gave her "the heebie-jeebies," and occasionally, when she was fed up, she let us know we were "really in the doghouse."

When anyone dropped something in the kitchen, they were "breaking up housekeeping," and when we pulled into the garage, which of course was often, she'd always say, reliably as the sun coming up, "Back the same day." She signed birthday cards in beautiful penmanship, always the same: Lovingly, Jessie.

When someone died, Jessie would say they passed over, and speak of how they were no longer in the body, or how they had given up the ghost. I pictured the spirit ghosts of people who died, wiggling out of their useless bodies, rising up and getting free, swimming through the air like we swam in the ocean. They died, but they were around. They were just no longer in the body. It was comforting.

I often think of Jessie's words, and sometimes speak them. I'm prone to using old-fashioned, reliable turns of phrase myself (just ask my sister), and have been known to proclaim "back the same day" as we pull into the garage. I frequently find myself humming. In the vibration I feel, more than hear, Jessie's voice inside me, a kind of playful sing song. It was soothing, the way she hummed and the way she spoke.

Jessie was reliable in many ways. When the house at La Atalaya burned, so did all the family pictures. We would have no photographic record of those early days in Del Mar if it weren't for Jessie. When World War II threatened and the Burnett family left Del Mar, Jessie wasn't about to leave her own precious belongings behind. So, along with getting Val ready to go, she bundled up her own things, her Bible with the white cover that zipped closed and her radio, her perfume bottles and kerchiefs, and the Shirley Temple doll and other mementos she'd saved from Valentine's childhood. And she did not forget her photograph albums. When Jessie died many years later and we were grieving her passing, it was an unexpected gift to discover the old photographs among her belongings.

Jessie in the 1930s

So our family's only pictorial history of La Atalaya in the 1920s and '30s is seen through Jessie's eyes, or those of a friend with a camera. Jessie lived at La Atalaya throughout the 1930s, and visited until the early '70s. Her bustling presence, her throaty chuckle, the velvety softness of her skin, her scolding that felt more like a hug, Jessie was at the center of my mother's early life.

And, as it turned out, the year Dwight D. Eisenhower was elected president, she returned to the center, this time helping to raise Val's kids. My brother Tim was a baby and I wasn't yet two when Jessie came to live with our family. And she was there 16 years later when I left for college.

Born in 1901, Jessie would have been 28 when she became Valentine's nurse, and 51 when she joined our family. The 1910 census lists Jessie Lela Wells as living with her mother, her brother Cecil and her grandmother in an apartment in Little Rock. There's no record of her father, and her mother seems to have disappeared after 1910.

There's no telling where Jessie met Houston, but by the time she was 18 they were married, launching her on a journey from Little Rock to St. Louis to Los Angeles to the Burnett family. Her promotion to caring for baby Valentine led her to Europe and the estate in Del Mar, to the chateau-style house at 104 Fremont Place, and eventually, to raising Val's kids too.

Jessie was an important member of the Burnett household, and not just for Val. In her album was a slightly dog-eared photo of herself sitting under a tree, with toddler Valentine in her lap and five-year-old Coy Jr. standing beside her, his hand resting on Jessie's shoulder. The closeness shared by the three of them is unmistakable, even in the faded sepia tones. The picture may have been taken by my grandmother. If so, it may be the only photo she took in Del Mar that survived the fire. No doubt she gave Jessie a copy, who then glued it onto one of the black paper pages in her photo album.

Coy Jr., Jessie and Val pose in a photo booth at a carnival.

In Grandmother's weekly letters to my Aunt King during World War II she gave updates about Jessie right along with family members, often revealing how much everyone relied on her.

Jessie and Val liked to dress up and have their picture taken.

Jessie may have still had family back in Little Rock, but the only one we ever heard about was "Brother Dear," which is how she referred to Cecil. And we only heard about him when he came around asking his sister for money. No, as far as we kids were concerned, Jessie had family – our family.

The rest of the grown-ups came and went, to work, to attend cocktail parties, to play cards or golf. They talked about politics and bridge hands and birdies and the state of the economy. They got in moods. They looked more like us kids than Jessie did, but we couldn't count on them. Through it all, there was Jessie, with her love of laughter and her skin the color of the "java" she liked so much, coffee laced with half and half, and plenty of sugar.

Along with saving Val's dolls and rare photo images of the original house on top of the hill at La Atalaya, Jessie was the keeper of our family's most tender secrets. When Val went off to UC Berkeley at the age of 16, Jessie continued as part of the Burnett staff. She was there when Val's brother, Coy Jr., collapsed in the attic at 104 Fremont Place and was taken in the ambulance to Good Samaritan Hospital.

King and Aunty Too rode with him in the ambulance, but they had to enter through the hospital's main entrance rather than the emergency room. When they got off the elevator they were met by the doctor, who told them young Coy had been pronounced dead. He had just turned 21.

A Different Story...

In the case of my uncle Coy, the tragedy of the loss of such a young man was compounded by its suddenness, and the mystery behind it. The death certificate alleged that he died of complications related to meningitis, which he had supposedly contracted when he was stationed in the Army in Oklahoma. So that was the official family story. At least among the grown-ups.

My cousin Dana - he who held us transfixed with whispered tales of Granddaddy's shady exploits from the past - had a different story to tell.

"It happened in the attic. He went up there after he told Granddaddy he was a homosexual, and Granddaddy told him to get out. And that's where they found him. Dead!"

Dana's flair for drama added spice to our family gatherings, dulled as they were by social propriety. Like many good tales, over the years Dana's changed. His story of our young uncle shooting himself in the head with a shotgun morphed into the more macabre image of Coy uncapping a gas line and breathing it in. Actually Charles Wild, the original owner of our grandparents' home at 104 Fremont Place, did kill himself just that way, upstairs in the attic, sucking on the gas line. It would be interesting to hear where exactly my cousin got his wild stories. But he's no longer with us.

Jessie's gone now, but her passing did not silence her. In fact, it was her death that revealed new information about Coy Jr., in the letter he wrote to her less than a year before he died – the letter that Jessie saved zipped into her Bible for us to find, more than 30 years later. Folded and refolded many times, the paper was fragile with age and wear. Perhaps she'd always had it with her.

It was addressed to "JeJe," a sweet baby name, and in it Coy entrusted her with a painful wish: "I want to go to God's land and join Maxine. I pray for this continually and if God is good to me, I will pass over very soon."

Young Coy assured her that he would not hurt himself, though he was deeply missing Maxine, a family friend who had died very young. Yet, along with the reassurance, he made his wishes clear and included letters he'd written to members of the family. He asked Jessie to safeguard them, and to distribute them after his death.

"But it's fine," he wrote, "if you want to read them."

There is no record of any letters the family may have received after Coy's death, let alone anyone's reaction to them. Even my mother, his sister, named as next of kin in Coy's military records and with whom he was very close, never spoke about a letter. Maybe for 17-year-old Valentine losing the only sibling she grew up with was enough to drive away clear memories of that terrible time.

* * *

Back in the glory days of La Atalaya, my grandparents employed a large number of people, and the space upstairs over the garages was needed for them. During Prohibition, one of the handymen who lived up there was making moonshine and blew up the still, not once but twice, apparently not an uncommon incidence in Del Mar during those years. The damage was repaired, and life went on.

In the 1950s and '60s, when La Atalaya was our vacation home, the adults in the family slept upstairs on the second floor, in the former staff quarters. There was only a small staff by then, and they slept in an area called the Blue Room and some other small rooms on the lower level, below the first floor. All of them, that is, except Jessie.

Jessie's bedroom was on the first floor, just down the hall from the kids' rooms, reassuringly close by. We never questioned this arrangement for a moment. We kids belonged to Jessie, and she to us.

While she wore stylish dresses during my mother's childhood, in the '50s and '60s Jessie often wore a white or occasionally pastel uniform, with stockings that she held up with rubber bands, just below her knees. On Sundays she dressed up for church, and when she went on vacations she wore regular clothes. She always smelled good, sweet coffee and the pomade she used to smooth her hair, maybe the scent of Jungle Gardenia or White Shoulders, her two favorite perfumes.

Jessie's skin was smooth and soft to touch, though we knew she had to use lots of lotions and creams, especially on her elbows and feet. She listened to radio stations that played hymns mostly. I liked to lie on her bed, on the white chenille bedspread, talking and listening to the music, playing with the little balls of cotton on the fabric and looking at all her things, so unlike my mother's things. I was intrigued with our differences and similarities, fascinated with the discovery that Jessie had a tan line when she took off her wristwatch, and reassured that when we turned up our palms, our skin pretty much matched.

Jessie enjoyed the radio, but she *loved* TV. And we loved it with her. The 1950s was the beginning of televisions in regular homes, and the first one that I remember well sat on a shelf suspended between metal rods that went from the floor to the ceiling, very mid-century modern. It was in the large family room on one end of our long ranch style house in Rolling Hills, but we didn't call it the family room. We called it the Playroom.

Windows ran along one wall of the Playroom, and on the opposite side sat the ironing board, where Jesse did sometimes iron. But mostly it served as her desk. She sat in a chair set up beside it, and would lean on the ironing board, presiding over us kids. She used it as a tray, too, it held her endless cups of sweet creamy coffee, and bowls of ice cream at night while we, she and we kids, watched TV. It was great to watch television with Jessie. She laughed and groaned much louder than our parents. She really got into the show, and that made it more fun.

Television in the 1950s and '60s was almost exclusively white. We were always on the lookout for a Black person in any show, and we would excitedly call Jessie to come see if she wasn't in the room. In the fall of 1968, the year I went off to college, there was a new weekly sitcom about a Black woman, a widow named Julia, who worked as a nurse and was raising her young son. It starred Diahann Carroll. Jessie loved that show. It was fun to come home from college and share her excitement about the first show ever featuring a Black woman professional.

The Civil Rights movement coincided with my growing from childhood into adolescence, both the times and my budding maturity heightening my awareness of racial discrimination. I felt confused. What did this mean about Jessie? Obviously she was not enslaved. She had a salary and, throughout the time I knew her, she always owned a home. But usually she lived at our house. I knew Jessie had fewer choices because of her skin color, because of racism. But I was so glad she lived with us. A baffling dilemma, it left me feeling sad and something worse, like being ashamed.

One afternoon, as Jessie and I were watching TV, the news showed a fashion show in Harlem called "Black Is Beautiful." Instead of going with the convention of the times, Black women straightening their hair and putting lightener on their skin, the Black models walking down the runway at the Harlem show all had dark skin and wore their hair natural. They looked beautiful. Free.

I was captivated. "Black Is Beautiful. I like that!" I looked at Jessie, hoping, I think, for approval. "I'm going to start saying it." It seemed so much better than calling people "colored."

Jessie wasn't convinced. She wouldn't really care to be called "Black," she said. "I like 'Negro.' It's more respectful."

I didn't know what to think.

Uncomfortable

I once tried to talk to my aunt King about my discomfort about Jessie's relationship to our family and to the history of our country.

"It's weird to think about Jessie being a servant. I know that's not the same as a slave or anything, but it seems wrong somehow."

Looking a bit bewildered, King replied, "Ever since she came to work for our family, Jessie has been a valued member of the staff. She has an important job and she does it well." I realized there was quite a difference in our perspectives, King born in 1916, I in 1950.

In addition to our generational differences, King experienced Jessie as a valued member of the team who helped keep the family running smoothly, like you'd think about valued employees in a company, while I experienced Jessie as a primary caregiver... as a mother. Maybe both of us were right in a way.

Martin Luther King was assassinated in the second semester of my senior year of high school. This loss of the inspirational man with a dream was shocking, frightening, a national trauma and tragedy. It underscored the profound significance of everything Dr. King stood for. Jessie just bowed her head. There were no words.

I wish she had lived to see Barack Obama become President. I wonder what she'd think about the term African American, or that barely anyone says "Negro" any more. We always knew her grandmother raised her, but if I could talk with Jessie now, I'd ask her if her grandmother, born in Mississippi in 1845, was free or enslaved in her early life. It is sobering to realize that the woman who raised us in the 1950s and '60s was likely raised by a woman who had experienced slavery.

I'd love to hear what it was like, becoming baby Valentine's nurse and going on a fabulous cruise to Europe, or living at La Atalaya when my mother was a girl. I'd be a little scared to ask, but I'd still want to know if Jessie regretted not having her own children. I'd be hoping we kids were enough.

I wonder what Jessie would think about Del Mar today. Would she share my sense of loss of the simpler times? Would she miss the Tudor-style Del Mar Hotel and the rickety beach shacks where now stand lovely homes? What would she say if I got nostalgic for the bookstore where I bought hardcover Nancy Drew mysteries for $1 plus 5 cents tax, or the old five-and-dime with its shelves full of something for everyone, including odd toys wrapped in crackly cellophane covered lightly in dust? So many changes, so much gone. She would likely purse her lips slightly, shaking her head at the loss.

But then, I think, Jessie would murmur something comforting and go about her business, humming.

When Jessie got sick at the end of her life, my mother visited her regularly, and when Jessie died, Mama took care of everything. She made sure that a large family who were close friends of Jessie's got all her things, and that her body was cremated. The ashes are in the same cemetery where my father was buried just a couple of years before. Jessie's ashes are not buried, but placed in the wall that surrounds a fountain. Visiting there and seeing her name on a small plaque set into the wall is made more memorable by the sound of water as it splashes and bubbles in the fountain. It's soothing. It reminds me of Jessie humming.

Jessie's Other Life

While we kids were shocked when we learned that Jessie and Houston were once married, we always knew that Jessie's life extended beyond our family. This was no mystery, because sometimes she included us in it.

There was her house in Fresno, several hours away from our home in Rolling Hills, where she had good friends and went on her vacations. Being kids we didn't pay attention to details that I'd love to ask about now, like when did she buy it, and why Fresno? Instead we just felt it was a treat to be there. For one thing, she had a player piano, something I never saw in anyone else's home. It sat against one wall of the cozy living room, with a collection of scrolls of perforated paper that could be loaded into the open place on the front, each scroll playing a different song. The scrolls had words running up one side so we could sing along while the piano played. There was "When the Saints Go Marching In," for instance, and "Blueberry Hill," which got on the Top 40, sung by Fats Domino. It was fun trying to sing along, but even more fun to watch the piano magically play itself.

In the guest room there were twin beds, where Claire and I slept when we stayed there, each bed with its own luxurious satiny comforter. One time, as a young teenager, I got to go with Jessie by myself. It was my early Beatles phase, and Jessie let me play my record over and over again, much louder than Mama would ever tolerate. We probably drove to Fresno in Jessie's secondhand convertible, which definitely would have added to the fun.

Later she sold that house, and bought a duplex in Southern California, in Watts. After we kids got to be teens, she moved out of our house and lived on one side of the duplex, but she wasn't alone. Although her old dog Hansi had died, he was followed by other dachshunds, first Pretzel, then a miniature named Schnitzel.

Jesse was a faithful churchgoer. Her church in Southern California, which she attended while she lived with us in Rolling Hills and later while she lived in Watts, was an altogether different experience than attending the Episcopalian services near our house. As far as I recall, the deacons were all women, Black women who called each other by their last names. So Jessie was Carter, which we thought was kind of funny. We felt welcomed at her church. It was full of spirited singing and praising and folks who seemed a lot happier to be there than the people did at St. Francis, where we usually went with Mama.

Jessie had a story about me and her friend Brunson, whose first name I never knew. I was little, about 3 years old, and I think we were visiting Brunson's house. She and Jessie had gone into the kitchen, and when Brunson came back into the living room to check on me I had apparently eaten a number of fancy chocolates from a gift box on the coffee table. According to the story, Brunson said "Oh, I don't think Jessie would like you to do that, Brier," and I responded, a chocolaty circle around my mouth, "Don't you say that to Brier! Don't you say that!"

Jessie always laughed telling that story, and I always felt happy, hearing it. She just had a way of making you feel good about yourself. Accepted, no matter what.

Chapter 20

Of the Sea, Part One

In the 1950s my family – my mother Val, my father Lloyd and we kids, and Jessie of course – started spending every August in Del Mar, and La Atalaya became ours. And while she didn't have the glamour of the original estate, she still had every bit of the charm. When summer came, we couldn't wait for August, couldn't wait to sleep in our garage-stall-shaped bedrooms. Because, except for sleeping, who wants to spend time in a bedroom when there's a whole world of adventures out there, just waiting for kids to come along and make them happen?

Like all children, we lived in our senses, and these were never more activated than during summers in Del Mar. Like the English translation of its name, we were *del mar* – "of the sea" – every bit as much as our favorite seaside town. And part of being *del mar* was being at the beach.

The 16th Street beach to be precise. There was a lifeguard in a raised wooden tower and a chalkboard with daily updates warning about rip tides and undertows. The sand was white and seemed the silkiest there,

Look out for rip tides! From left to right: Tim, Pat, Jessie, our cousin Neal, and Claire

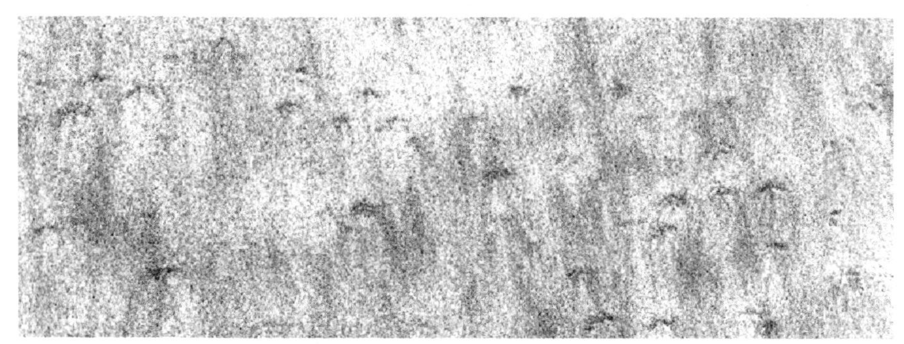

Crab V's in the wet sand at Del Mar

sometimes with a thin crust of dried salt water. In the mornings we liked to crunch the fragile surface with our feet. The sand would squish up between our toes in crisp powdery puffs as we ran to the water.

The wet sand was a popular home for sand crabs. Every wave brought more of them body surfing into shore. The waves would slide back out to sea, revealing dozens of little crabs suspended on the sand. They'd freeze for a split second and then start digging frantically, wiggling around our toes as they burrowed themselves into the moist sand. V-shaped patterns would appear along the sand's glistening surface, as the water receded around the crab bumps. Between waves the sunlight would sparkle on the uneven rows of V's as they melted away, finally leaving no trace.

There were V's overhead too, each one a seagull circling, screeching out their presence as they looked for food. The sand crabs were dead meat if they didn't wiggle down into the sand fast.

Standing there in the cool shallow water – seagulls soaring overhead, our toes tickled by the waves, the sun hot on our faces as it moved into the afternoon – was enough to fill a whole day. We played poison waves, which required us to jump over waves or be killed. Double waves were the real challenge. Another favorite game was statues, standing frozen along the foamy edge of the waves as the sand slowly built into soft wet mounds around our feet until they, like the sand crabs, would disappear completely. We could stand there for a long time, up to our ankles in wet sand, staring out at the far horizon and trying to imagine we could (almost) see Japan, or at least Hawaii. We had no idea how far away those places might be, but figured it couldn't be much farther than where the blue water, which stretched before us to the west without limit, seemed to fall off the edge of the world. We'd agree, we could understand why all those people in the olden days thought the earth was flat.

If we came in the morning, which we usually did if the weather was good, which it usually was, we were often the first people at the beach. Jessie would set up the umbrella and herself under it, on a tatami mat in the shade, with her dachshund, Hansi, curled up beside her. Mama would place a low beach chair in the sun, put on her dark glasses and read gossip magazines about Hollywood stars. This indulgence was saved exclusively for Del Mar. She usually wore a two-piece bathing suit, her stomach bulging slightly as she sat reading, and the sun would gradually leave a brown stripe across her middle. Every summer it was the same; the glossy tabloids and that stripe of tan were as reliable as the ocean's tides.

Jessie and Pat sit in the shade of the umbrella while the older kids enjoy the sand and sea, supervised by Jessie's dog, Hansi.

We kids wasted no time staying on shore; we'd race down to the water to see who could get there first, discarding our thongs and any other encumbrances willy-nilly as we ran across the sand. Before the afternoon swimmers showed up, we could stand in the shallow waves looking out and believe we were the only ones in the world. Sometimes it was hard to remember we weren't.

If we went later in the day, we'd watch the sun set over the ocean, and imagine it like a cartoon, a hot ball of fire sinking into the water. We never saw the horizon start bubbling and boiling in some Disneyesque fashion, but on a really hot day it seemed like it could happen.

As a young teenager, standing in the waves wasn't that different than when I was a child, but instead of being the place to imagine the world like a cartoon, the ocean provided a retreat into fantasies about growing up. The crash of the waves was a welcome cover to singing Beatles songs at the top of my lungs, while I imagined dating Paul and knowing all the right things to say. No matter what age I was, the beach at Del Mar was the best place on earth to be.

Sometimes clouds would begin to build up in the afternoon until they were thick over the sea, reaching up and swallowing the sun whole before it reached the horizon. The wind would pick up, chilly against our freshly burnished skin, and the afternoon would suddenly become gray and boring. Those are the only afternoons we'd be quick picking up our shovels and buckets and towels and rafts, and finding our other thong (one was always missing) so we could go home.

If we hadn't swallowed too much salt water we'd be very hungry when we got home from the beach. They say that hunger is the best spice, but we discovered that hunger *after a day at the beach* is the best. Food never tasted better than it did then. Hot dogs with yellow mustard. Cold fried chicken. Oreos by the handfuls with a cold glass of milk. The sensory pleasures of Del Mar never ran out.

When Mama was busy, Houston drove us to the beach in the old limousine, the one with the bulbous shape and cracking leather seat covers, not like Granddaddy's new one with the pointy fins and soft gray upholstery. Jessie would ride beside him in the front seat and we kids would climb into the back. Our half flat rubber rafts went into the trunk, and our first stop was the gas station, so we could blow them up. That trunk seemed as big as a room, but after the rafts were filled with air they'd be too fat to fit, so we'd pile them into the space between the front and back seats of the limo, like the mattresses between the princess and the pea. Sometimes Tim or Pat would get to ride in front, while the other one would press the button in back that made the privacy window go up and down, over and over again, behind Houston's head. They'd press the intercom button and use it too. Since Mama wasn't there, nobody made them stop.

At the beach rafts were fun, but we preferred body surfing, even though every summer each of us kids wiped out at least a few times. A wipeout starts with a promising swell of ocean, just like any good bodysurfing wave. But then there's another swell behind it, bigger, faster; suddenly it catches up to the first swell, turning it into a giant wave. As we'd start down the big slide of water, hoping for a smooth long ride all the way to shore, the wave would become a giant foamy hand, reaching up and pulling us under. The salt water rushed up our noses and into our mouths as the wave ground us down into the sand at the bottom of the ocean, making for a very scary moment before we got back up to the surface, spitting and sputtering, the salt water stinging our eyes as we took big gulps of air.

Since he was a daredevil, and the littlest, Pat had some of the worst wipeouts. But no matter how bad they looked, he'd always pop back up like a cork, grinning.

"I meant to do that!"

In spite of the annual wipeouts, we found that facing the waves and deciding which ones were good for riding, and which ones we needed to dive beneath or thrust ourselves through, held endless fascination and challenge. The only thing better was when Papa was at the beach.

Because of his work, our father, Lloyd, was not able to spend much time in Del Mar, at least not nearly as much as his kids would have liked. Because Papa was fun! And Papa at the beach was the most fun of all, especially when one of us got to go out deep with just him and a raft. The lucky kid would ride the raft while our father pushed from behind. Only with him would we venture beyond where the waves formed, where not even he could touch. He'd push the raft to make us sail over the swells, waiting, waiting, until the perfect wave started to form, way out in the deep. Papa would turn our raft toward shore as the wave approached, and with a single huge shove he would send the raft up and over the bank of water as it turned into a mountainous wave, with the kid-bearing raft flying down the side, like a toboggan on snow. No matter how far out we'd go, he seemed to know how to pick just the right wave that would take us all the way to shore.

We built sandcastles, hundreds of them through the years, with underground rooms and secret passageways, deep water-filled moats with bridges, and columns made of wet sand carefully, patiently, dripped, one gritty drop at a time, into tall spindly turrets that made them really look like castles. When that was finished we'd decorate the castle, which involved careful hunting and gathering of shells and seaweed and any other decorative objects, natural or otherwise, that we might find in the sand.

Unlike the shells they sold at the beach stores along the Pacific Coast Highway on the way down from L. A., the shells in Del Mar weren't glamorous or giant-sized. Most of them were small, and often many were broken, so finding intact shells required careful searches. Our favorites were the ones we called angel shells, shaped like little wings. It didn't really count to find a single one – there were loads of those everywhere, and every wave washed in a few more. We were pickier than that. The ones we collected had to be attached pairs, two little shells linked together, making a perfect set of angel wings. They came in pinks and violets and oranges. My favorites were the yellow-and-white-striped ones; they looked like someone had painted them very carefully, and never went outside the lines once. When I stroked them they felt as creamy as they looked. Almost edible.

Angel shells

So the prized double angel shells were placed in the most important spots of the sandcastle, along with the rubbery brown "budfloats" of seaweed sticking out like weapons along the top of the castle. The long slippery brown "leaves" of the seaweed could be draped across to make a roof over the open parts of the castle. If we built our castle in the morning, when we first got there, by the time we left in the late afternoon the seaweed would have been cooking all day in the sun, with a smell like concentrated ocean. Fishy, salty, strangely wonderful, the smell engulfed us as we carefully removed the angel shells, to add to our growing collection back at La Atalaya.

When we came back the next morning the castle would be all gone, melted into a lump in the sand if it was huge, but usually leaving no sign that it had ever been there at all. Such total disappearance whispered to us, not so much about impermanence as about magic.

The waves were reliable that way. They never let us down, magically clearing off the beach each night so we could start fresh every morning, making new footprints in perfectly smoothed-out, slightly crunchy sand that stretched forever along the deserted tan-and-white beach, encircled by the indigo sea and the blue bowl of sky overhead.

Just for a Moment

The gulls above crying their lonely call, the sand crabs under my toes, the breeze drying my skin to a salty crust, fresh and slightly astringent . . . the taste and sound and smells of any oceanside setting transport me back to my childhood as reliably as the magic of the waves. The memories are mine to keep.

There I am without a care in Del Mar, just for a moment, before I remember this is a different time and place, and that our property there was gone from us long ago and belongs to another family entirely.

Chapter 21

The Turf Club

Every afternoon at two o'clock sharp, from Tuesday through Saturday, the melodious voice of Bing Crosby singing "Where the Turf Meets the Surf" rang out across the slough, echoed through the river valley, and then climbed up the hill to where we kids could hear it from our house. This meant the American Thoroughbred horse-racing track in Del Mar was open for the day. We could even glimpse the track from our yard up on the ridge, around the bend to the north. But it was too far away to really make out what was going on there.

Bing wasn't there in person, at least not most of the time. But his song welcoming all listeners to Del Mar, that special place, was as reliable a part of those August days as the waves breaking on the beach or Jessie's favorite sayings. The second we heard Bing crooning, his voice a little tinny with the scratchy old recording, we knew that Grandmother and Granddaddy were settling in to watch the races begin. They'd be seated in their private box at the Turf Club, next to Hollywood celebrities, fellow tycoons and other successful people who chose to watch the races from a comfortable height, rather than mingle with the crowds standing in the open areas along the racetrack below. Each private box had comfortable chairs around a dining table covered in white linen, set with heavy silverware, and laden with china plates of tasty food, served by formally dressed waiters.

It was no fluke that Bing's song welcomed visitors. The day the Del Mar Thoroughbred Club opened in 1937, Bing himself was at the gate greeting and shaking hands with every person who entered. He wasn't just a pretty voice or well-known face. The concept and ultimately the manifestation of horse racing in Del Mar was the result of a business partnership between Bing Crosby and others, including other Hollywood stars Pat O'Brien and Oliver Hardy.

Racetracks had come to Southern California during the Depression, after Proposition 5 passed in 1933, legalizing pari mutuel wagering on horseracing. Within three months of its passing, the first track opened, and several others quickly followed, everyone anxious to get in on the action. The track at Santa Anita, which opened on Christmas Day, 1934 was cutting-edge – the first Thoroughbred racetrack anywhere to install photo-finish cameras. Folks were eager for excitement and distraction during those hard times of the 1930s, and horse racing was becoming very popular, for a time rivaling baseball as the nation's favorite spectator sport.

My grandparents bought the house in Del Mar and developed La Atalaya years before Bing and company built their racetrack. So were they excited when construction began down the hill beside the county fairgrounds, or worried it would be a noisy nuisance? Maybe it was because of the track at Del Mar that they got interested in horse races in the first place.

Maybe Granddaddy was drawn to horse racing in the late 1930s, and the Tuna Club on Catalina in the '20s, because he was making a name for himself, and these were the places to be. Or maybe it was his love of horses, dating back to his early days as a boy on the farm in Nebraska and the job caring for lawyer Starr's prize horses, the job that launched his legal career. Maybe he just loved to gamble. He certainly liked the science of

DEL MAR HISTORICAL SOCIETY ARCHIVES

Bing Crosby greets guests on opening day at the Del Mar Thoroughbred Club

betting, carefully scrutinizing each day's *Racing Form*, with its small print and rows and rows of tiny numbers, racing statistics he'd circle and underline with his own notation system.

By 1950, the year I was born, my grandparents were in their mid-60s, and by the time I was paying any attention they were well entrenched in their late-life patterns. In summer those patterns centered on horse racing in Southern California: Santa Anita, Hollywood Park and Del Mar.

Off to the Races

The earliest story I know about our family's attachment to horse racing dates from the late 1940s, when my parents were getting married. My father's 17-year-old sister Lois, who was in the wedding party, came from northern California to stay at 104 Fremont Place, an experience she recalls as being one of the most exciting weeks of her life. She never forgot the time the bride invited her to go shopping. They hopped into Valentine's red two-door roadster and took off, on the hunt for a pair of shoes. After going to a number of stores, Lois was relieved when Val finally found a pair she liked, but her relief turned to disbelief when Valentine, a worldly 19, said she liked the style and fit, so bought the shoes in every color available.

Lois remembers that later that week Granddaddy treated her to a day at the track at Santa Anita with all the trimmings: riding in the limousine, the plush surroundings, tiny jockeys in colorful silks atop beautiful horses, the excitement of seeing celebrities, and of course, the races themselves.

We kids got to go to the races at Del Mar once each summer. My grandparents went to the track every day of the Del Mar racing season. My grandmother would be wearing one of her numerous signature hats. Underneath she wore a fancy black net intended to disguise her ever thinning gray hair, but you could still make out the pink scalp peeking through it. She'd have on jewelry, usually large costume jewelry. Very good costume jewelry. Grandmother had style, and, being born in 1887, she came into that style in the early 20th century, a time when women – society "ladies" and factory "girls" alike – had a wardrobe of accessories, with a hat, stockings and gloves for every season, and, if they had the means, maybe a parasol for the sun and an elaborate fan for evening galas. The Twenties brought looser standards, and, along with being granted their long-awaited right to vote, women started wearing looser garments, freeing themselves from their corsets, smelling salts and fainting couches. But my grandmother's style was set before those freedoms: slim dresses and fitted coats, nylons, black net gloves. And, always, a hat.

Don't get me wrong. Grandmother was fashionable, never dowdy. Her clothing was beautifully made. She loved fine fabrics and fine craftsmanship. One summer, in the mid '60s, she came downstairs to leave for the track dressed in a short-skirted "mod" dress with a geometric black-and-white print that she wore with patterned stockings and short white leather boots. Courrèges boots, Mama called them, by a famous French designer. Watching my aged grandmother getting into the limousine I was in awe. Those boots were just like ones I'd seen on *The Dick Clark Show,* on go-go dancers my own age, doing The Pony in cages hanging from the ceiling on either side of the stage. I felt quite envious of my grandmother's stylish look; as a teen I was way too self-conscious to pull it off, inhibited by the image of unattainable perfection. Grandmother had exquisite linen jackets and cashmere wraps, and in the cooler months she often wore fur coats. And no matter what she wore, everyone other than family addressed her as "Mrs. Burnett." Even my grandfather did, in public.

She'd depart for the track with Granddaddy, who would look every bit the part of the successful businessman, always in a suit and tie, the day's Racing Form tucked under his arm. Surrounded by his estate, he'd say hello to Houston and climb into their latest Cadillac. These were personal limousines, aesthetically pleasing. The size of a very long station wagon, with the back door opening into a large carpeted area between the very comfortable back seat and the front seat, the car was spacious but not "stretched."

After Bing's trademark song, while the horses were still parading around to show themselves off, the classic racetrack bugle call would sound, the horn as tinny as Bing's voice. The crowd would grow louder with anticipation, people rushing past to place a last-minute bet, scrambling to find a good spot to see the action, yelling for a friend. Then everyone would go silent, momentarily frozen, waiting for the horses to burst out of the gates and surge down the track, the jockeys' arms pumping up and down as they brandished their short whips. People would start waving their arms and shouting encouragement to their horse while they stood on tiptoe to see.

Up in the Turf Club my grandparents quietly and unhurriedly settled in. They didn't have to scramble for a good view. They, of course, had a great view.

The record of Bing's voice may have been scratchy, but the opening song still seemed to transport his cheerful presence to Del Mar each afternoon. It helped us imagine the excitement of the late 1930s and '40s as movie stars flocked to the newly popular resort town of Del Mar. The nontraditional opening time, at 2 o'clock, an hour later than most racetracks opened, was specifically chosen to coordinate with the train schedule, for folks traveling south from Hollywood.

A year after it opened, in a move that helped put the fledgling racetrack on the map, the Del Mar Thoroughbred Club hosted a $25,000 winner-take-all match race between two horses, Ligaroti, owned by Bing himself, and Seabiscuit, who would later become a legend. The race was widely publicized and discussed and was one of the first nationwide radio broadcasts of a Thoroughbred race. Although there's been controversy about it since, Seabiscuit won the race by a nose. But Bing's horse was still a big win for the famous crooner, because it helped put Del Mar on the horse-racing map.

The song about the turf meeting the surf was still playing in the 1960s, but by then it was harder to hear it from La Atalaya, competing as it did with our blasting plastic transistor radios. They were tuned to the closest rock-and-roll station, across the border to the south. Between the Top 40 tunes, the station's call letters would ring out in Spanish, with music playing in the background like you might hear at a bullfight: XTRA Tijuana Mexico!

In the evenings at La Atalaya we'd hang out in the living area on the first floor (the children's level), sprawled on the worn couch and day bed. The nights were usually warm, so the windows would all be open, the crickets providing a background chorus to whoever was singing on the transistor. One summer when our older cousins were there, it was a lot of Beatles and Bob Dylan. Anne's daughter Durrie, only a few years older than I was, seemed light-years ahead of me, talking about dating with her close friend Donna, who was actor Donald O'Connor's daughter. Listening to their stories about going to parties and meeting rock-and-roll stars left me feeling awkward and naïve.

Our oldest cousin, Durrie's brother John, was home on a break from the Marines. It was scary, like so many things during the Vietnam war, the way he'd suddenly turned into a full-fledged man, a real grown-up. He said he was in Del Mar for some "R and R." He seemed nice, but serious. One evening he spent a long time explaining the meaning of Dylan's "Like a Rolling Stone" to me. I appreciated that, so I didn't tell him I still wasn't sure I got it.

Although we were much more interested in the latest Beatles record than the rising fame of jockey Willie Shoemaker, it was still fun for us kids to go to the races each year. We'd clean up and put on nice clothes, then squish our feet into shoes that suddenly seemed at least a size too small. We'd get into the limo and ride with our grandparents down and around the hill, for our day at the track.

On this occasion, Granddaddy would ride in front with Houston, doubtless putting as much distance as possible between himself and four lively grandchildren. We'd scramble into the back. Tim and Patrick would pull out the jump seats that folded down from the back of the front seat, examining them before sitting down, always intrigued with anything engineered. Grandmother might let them turn on the small reading lights or raise the window behind Houston's head, and even use the speaker. As far as I know, the boys were the only ones who ever deployed that barrier and communication system; Granddaddy never used it. Claire and I would position ourselves between Mama and Grandmother, on the comfy passenger seat covered in plush dove-gray wool flannel. I could smell Grandmother's Chanel #5 and Mama's Joy perfume blending together as I smoothed down my dress and rubbed my palm along the velvety upholstery.

Once there, Houston pulled right up to the entrance, and a man wearing a red cap and jacket opened the back door for us. We'd step out of the shiny black limo like celebrities, though of course we knew we were just beach kids dressed up for a day with our grandparents.

We would follow behind Grandmother and Granddaddy, getting a kick out of how they were treated like royalty. Bowing over her gloved hand, a man dressed like a maître d' would solemnly welcome "Mrs. Burnett." Then, gravely, he would offer Mr. Burnett his daily tip sheets and the *Racing Form*, which my grandfather would accept with a pleasant nod even though we knew he had another one in his pocket, covered with his cryptic notations in the margins.

After we settled in, Granddaddy would give us dimes with which to wager bets among ourselves at the table. We'd feel a collective thrill as the horses, mounted by the diminutive, colorful jockeys, entered the gates. The announcer's deep, somber voice would come over the loudspeakers: "Ladies and gentlemen, the horses are ready for the running of the first race..." The crowd would go quiet, there'd be the loud pop!, the gates would suddenly swing open and they were off!

Soon after the first race we'd order lunch, the waiters making a little fuss over us kids, especially Pat, drawn to his curly-haired naughtiness. I'd usually order a club sandwich (which into adulthood I thought was named for the Del Mar Turf Club). The fancy china plates and thick linen napkins seemed to make the double-decker sandwich – with toast, not bread – taste even better. Because it was a special occasion, we were allowed to order kiddie cocktails, Shirley Temples. A man would bring the tall glasses, clinking with ice and fizzing red with the little pop of 7Up and grenadine. At the Turf Club they decorated Shirley Temples with an orange slice and maraschino cherries stuck on little paper parasols, making them a highlight of our annual treat. We'd save the tiny parasols, which folded like umbrellas, for later play. Usually they ended up being used to stab one another. For fun, of course.

In addition to play-betting with dimes, we kids got to pick one race, out of the daily nine, on which to place a real bet. We'd each decide whether our bet was to win, place or show, and then my grandfather would go purchase the tickets for $2.00 apiece. Never one to enjoy the thrill of gambling, I'd always go for the safe odds and choose a "show" ticket, to up the chances that I'd win whether the horse came in first, second or third.

One year there was a horse running with "Valentine" as part of its name. In a show of support for the horse that was my mom's namesake, and in spite of the fact that the horse was deemed a real long shot, we each bought a ticket to win, including Granddaddy, who went to the window to place the bets. The final odds were something like 30 to 1 when the pistol shot off and the horses burst out of the gates. Clutching our tickets, we cheered to see Valentine keeping up with the faster horses as the race progressed. We were screaming by the time they moved into the final stretch, when we saw our horse inch ahead. It was a photo finish. Granddaddy took us all downstairs where we could see the glossy black-and-white, eight-by-ten photographs of the finish, where they were posted on the wall in a glass cabinet right after the race.

Valentine won by a nose. Each of us kids got an unimaginable fortune – $60! I don't know about my grandfather. I hope he made a killing with that bet from the heart.

Aside from Grandmother's clothes, my grandparents were not chic or trendy; they were old and set in their ways. But they loved going to the horse races, and in doing so they joined some of Hollywood's best known celebrities.

Crosby and O'Brien weren't the only Hollywood celebrities that frequented the track. Jimmy Durante was also a regular, and was still there in the 1950s, a fixture, sipping on a cup of coffee and studying a tip sheet. His nose actually looked bigger in person, if that's possible. When we kids worked up the nerve to ask him, he'd give us his autograph on a discarded ticket or program. He was always nice about it.

The nicest Hollywood star I ever met there was a giant of a man who, seeing me picking up the discarded tickets we kids liked to collect to play "races," offered me a handful of worthless Daily Double tickets that cost $20 apiece. Ouch! I looked up from the large hand holding the tickets. Walter Matthau did not look terribly disappointed about his losses. Instead he seemed interested, delighted to hear how excited my little brother would be over this treasure trove. Pulling a face, he said, "Well, I'm glad they're worth something to somebody."

Just above my grandparents' box in the Turf Club sat the Arnaz family: Lucy and Desi and their two children, Lucie and Desi Jr. Their family also had a place in Del Mar, on the beach, and also liked the track. Having grown up, as so many of us did, on side-splitting episodes of *I Love Lucy,* we were excited to recognize Lucille Ball the first time. With time this became ordinary. I found there was something I didn't like about young Lucie, close to my age, but maybe just because her parents were famous.

Rather than looking at celebrities, my sister, Claire, and I preferred to go to the fancy, fragrant Ladies' powder room, where we'd sit on tufted stools in front of the beveled mirrors. The long dressing table held a vast assortment of powders and perfumes we could actually apply. Sometimes we were having so much fun we'd miss a race or two.

Sitting in the Turf Club offered us the experience we would need later on to see through the power and wealth and celebrity worship that has increasingly dominated our society in recent years. I'm glad I saw early that rich or famous people are really just people like the rest of us, only they're famous or rich. Some are kind, some selfish. Some seem to transcend their favored status while others need to believe in their own mythology.

It was a lot of fun, that one day each summer, to dress up and rub elbows with the elite at the Turf Club. But we were always glad, the next day, to put our bathing suits back on, still a little sandy in the crotch, slip on our thongs and head down to the beach, where everyone sat on towels and had to look out for rip tides and undertows and seemed pretty much the same as us.

My grandmother, Mildred Kingsbury Burnett, at the Del Mar Turf Club

DEL MAR HISTORICAL SOCIETY ARCHIVES

Chapter 22

The Blue Room

When Houston wasn't chauffeuring my grandparents, he was usually relaxing in the Blue Room. The former garages at La Atalaya, the building with the red tile roof, had three levels, two floors above ground and one below. Because the house was built on a steep grade, the lowest level was cut into the hillside, with the back below ground level. But it had its own windows and walk-out in the front. A set of stairs, concrete of course, ran down the side of that floor into the lower courtyard, which served as the drying area. This was a large open space with a concrete floor and tall walls between which stretched massive clotheslines, used mostly for hanging out bedding and towels and other large pieces of laundry.

Off the drying yard a door opened into a large room with windows and a couple of doors leading to other spaces beyond. In the earlier days of the estate, when the staff was larger, this served as just one part of the servants' quarters, the others being a space in the main house and the large second floor over the garages. In the 1950s though, this one small area was where the cook, the chauffeur and sometimes other servants stayed during the summer season. Why it was called the Blue Room remains, like Aunty Too's nickname, a mystery.

The Chicken House

In the middle of the drying yard was a single chaise lounge where Granddaddy liked to sunbathe in the mornings or late afternoons. Growing up with Jessie, I was accustomed to differences in skin color, but it was still a shock to see the color of our wrinkled old grandfather wearing just a pair of baggy shorts, lying on a sheet draped over a chaise lounge. The scene gave "white" a whole new meaning. It was as if Granddaddy's natural skin color was camouflage for blending nearly invisibly into the sheet beneath him and the concrete surrounding him, all in various shades of whiteness.

My sister and I would lean out the small window in the "chicken house" up the hill, high above the drying yard below, and spy on him lying down there, equally fascinated and repelled by the sight. His prone body on the sheet-covered chaise looked small and defenseless - inexplicably, in spite of sunbathing, never tanner. There hadn't been chickens in the chicken house since the fire, but Claire and I spent hours playing in its musty upstairs room. For a period we spent a lot of time being Anne Frank, hiding from the Nazis. When he was out there, we worked Granddaddy's presence into our play drama.

We kids sometimes visited the Blue Room. Did Houston or the others who lived there mind hearing our footsteps clomp down the stairs, signaling as they did our intrusion into their personal area? Looking into that dim, too-small space, I could see its metal-framed beds for the men pushed against the walls, with a table beside each, and a large table with chairs around it in the middle of the main room. The two doors off this central area led to a bathroom and one small private bedroom, for the women. There was nowhere to get away.

It's hard now to imagine that Houston or others didn't resent us. They seemed welcoming, but maybe because they thought they had to be, as servants. Oblivious to these social implications, we kids just knew we liked to hang out down there. It was interesting and fun to be around grown-ups who were different.

Houston was playful and liked to laugh, in stark contrast to our grandfather's somber persona. After his legs were amputated, it was hard for him to get up and down the stairs to the Blue Room. We spent more time down there after that. The stairs and drying yard were in the sun, but the Blue Room, tucked into the lower corner of the building, was always cool and dim, less servants' quarters than desirable mystery space, at least to us kids.

Eventually a little electric track was installed along the concrete steps leading down to the Blue Room, with a chair that rode up and down like the one that ran up the back stairs at my grandparents' house in Fremont Place. It was like a tiny train, and we all had fun when we got to ride the stair chair, and felt lucky when it was our turn. But usually it was reserved for Houston.

The "Don't Talk" Rule

When we kids learned that Houston and Jessie had once been married, it was like finding out the impossible had happened. Jessie, married to Houston? Divorced?? What? How? When? Our predictable world was shaken off its axis as we tried to imagine Jessie being divorced. It was hard enough to imagine her being married, although she was supposedly married to a man named Mr. Carter, whom we never met or heard anything about. But she was called Mrs. Carter by her neighbors when we visited her house.

So Jessie was a married woman, or maybe a widow. But divorced? Impossible! Back then we did not know anyone who got divorced, and that it would be Jessie, the most religious person we knew, was mind-boggling. We never spoke about this with her. It was just too weird.

Do most families not talk about such important things? Was it my mother's family ethnicity, the stiff-upper-lip-ness of British heritage, or the classism and politeness that captured us all in our roles? Did all that privilege bring some special admonition, "Do not share anything intimate"?

For instance, the summer we arrived to find Houston in his wheelchair, legless, I stood tongue-tied, afraid of saying something wrong. Even as a child I was an anxious practitioner of the "Don't Talk" rule, picking up on the family tradition of favoring pleasantry over intimacy.

My earliest instruction in this rule took place in the car on Christmas day, on the way to my grandparents' house in Fremont Place for the family dinner. I was 5 years old. Mama told us that our Uncle John, her sister Anne's husband, had died. Not only that, he had killed himself by taking too many sleeping pills.

"Everyone is very upset. You must be careful not to talk about it," our mother cautioned us. "That way we can all try to enjoy being together for Christmas."

This warning was ringing in my ears as we approached my grandparents' house at 104 Fremont Place, the big fancy double doors looming ahead. Once inside, we saw the sweeping staircase beautifully festooned with a long garland of evergreens, but even though it was one of my favorite smells of the season, I couldn't enjoy the crisp tang of the pine.

What if I accidentally say something? I worried to myself. *What if I don't even mean to, but it just comes out . . . ?*

As we made our way into the living room with the grand piano and towering Christmas tree, undoubtedly decorated by the staff, I could think of no other topic than Uncle John's death. Not even the presents under the tree or my favorite holiday treat, the macadamia nuts from Hawaii, covered in powdered salt, which sat in a silver dish on the library table every Christmas, could distract me from thinking about what I was supposed to not say. I don't know how well we did following the "Don't talk" rule during that difficult Christmas visit, but I do know the caution to keep it pleasant or say nothing at all was branded forever into my brain.

I have spent a lifetime trying to unlearn it and to become as free as my little brother Patrick, bluntly asking Houston what happened to his legs. It motivated me in becoming a family therapist. I so yearned to break the rule and help people really talk with one another, that I came to make a living doing so.

Sometimes my role includes helping folks remember their youthful wisdom, when they weren't afraid to risk crossing barriers that divide us, or to say what we aren't supposed to say.

Chapter 23

The Last Train to Clarksville

In 1966, Del Mar got a new name. It lasted for just one day, but that was all part of the fun. To understand how Del Mar found herself at the center of a teenage treasure hunt of sorts and got a brand new name requires a look back to the popular music scene of the later 1960s.

"The Sixties" in America was a time of revolution, complete with an invasion by the British. Unlike the earlier revolution in U. S. history, however, this time the country welcomed the British invaders, in the form of rock groups that dominated the music charts for a decade. Of those groups, none was so record-breaking, so musically gifted, so influential, as the Fab Four. Or as they were better known, The Beatles.

The Beatles arrived on U. S. soil in February, 1964, following weeks of eager anticipation. Newspaper headlines, playing on the invasion theme, screamed "The Beatles Are Coming! The Beatles Are Coming!" Their appearance on *The Ed Sullivan Show* on February 9 brought them into people's living rooms, where 73 million people watched the shaggy foursome set the audience into near frenzy singing "She Loves You." Every "Woooo!" in the chorus brought louder screams. Yeah! Yeah! Yeah!

A couple of other acts were unfortunate enough to be scheduled to perform alongside the Beatles that night, little remembered as sharing a stage with the new musical sensation. The audience did muster a degree of enthusiasm when one of the performers sang a number from the hit musical *Oliver!* The song was "I'd Do Anything" and the singer was a former jockey, named Davy Jones. Two-and-a-half years later, he would become central to the mystery that changed Del Mar's name.

The Beatles were an unprecedented phenomenon. After *The Ed Sullivan Show* they went on a world tour, from Denmark to Hong Kong to New Zealand. Later in 1964 they returned to the United States, performing in a tour of 26 cities that stretched across the country and back again. Between tours, they made a movie, supposedly depicting a single day in the life of four Liverpudlians. *A Hard Day's Night,* with its goofy, farcical plot that included Paul's fictional grandfather, "a clean old man," was another first in The Beatles' story, a success with the critics and at the box office.

My first Beatles album was *Please Please Me*, wrapped in red paper, its desirability dwarfing other presents under the Christmas tree that year. I loved the harmonica in "Love Me Do" and the raucous call to "Twist and Shout." I practiced dancing to that song, and my Chubby Checker record, so often that I actually won a twist contest at one of our "Coke Dances" in Junior High. As teenagers in Del Mar listening to Beatles music being broadcast over the Mexican border, we'd debate which song was sung by Paul, which by John.

In August of '64 we didn't want to wait to get back to Los Angeles to see the Fab Four's new movie, so we talked Mama into taking us to the Solana Theatre just north of Del Mar, in Solana Beach. It was old-fashioned, and still had a room glassed in at the back of the theater called the Crying Room, where parents with young children could enjoy the movie without bothering others.

Standing in line to buy tickets for *A Hard Day's Night,* Mama remembered the theater from her childhood. "It only cost a nickel for a double feature. And there weren't regular seats back then, just wooden benches we'd sit on."

Mid-century Los Angelinos, we kids were shocked by this level of rusticity.

"Wooden benches without backs?"

"Wasn't it really uncomfortable?"

"Well, not to us. It was always exciting to go to the movies. And we could bring our dogs, as long as they behaved. It was different then."

We got our tickets and settled into our seats, grateful they weren't slabs of wood.

The summer of 1965 was a time of unrest in Los Angeles, with racial tensions erupting into the Watts Riots in early August. But we were self-absorbed teenagers, tucked safely away in Del Mar for the month, and we knew Jessie, who had a house in Watts, was safe with us. What drew our attention wasn't the terrible housing discrimination that had plagued Hispanic and Black families for decades in L. A. It was the fact that the Beatles were back on tour in the United States.

Then we found out that on the evening of August 28th, John, Paul, George and Ringo would be at Balboa Stadium in San Diego. We knew how close that was; we'd gone to the San Diego Zoo several times. We begged Mama to take us to the concert. In an effort to persuade, we told her the tickets were very reasonable – three levels at just $5.50, $4.50 and $3.50.

So that's how Valentine, a middle-aged woman with a preference for piano bars and show tunes, came to be sitting at a rock-and-roll concert with her four children, ages 9 to 14, and 17,000-plus other people, singing along to the music we had all come to know so well. It was a late decision to add San Diego to the concert schedule, and in spite of Beatlemania and a record-breaking crowd of over 55,000 at the brand new Shea Municipal Stadium in Queens, New York earlier that month, the show in San Diego wasn't even sold out.

It opened with a number of short performances, by people we'd never heard of. We squirmed around. It was nearly impossible to be patient. Then Cannibal and the Headhunters took the stage and our restlessness turned to excitement. It was fitting that a group of young musicians out of the housing projects in East L. A. opened the show in Southern California, welcoming the Beatles with the sound of Chicano Rock. We were all up on our feet as the band broke into "Land of 10,000 Dances," singing "Naa Na Na Na Naa ..."

And then – The Beatles!

From their opening version of "Twist and Shout" to the more obscure "Dizzy Miss Lizzy" and "Everybody's Trying to Be My Baby," they put on a great show. It was a relatively tame crowd, especially for a Beatles concert. From our seats in the $4.50 section we could actually hear the songs and kind of make out who was singing. It was thrilling!

By the following year, Beatles fever had reached epidemic proportions. Their concerts turned into near riots of swooning, crying, screaming fans. In August of 1966, some friends and I joined 45,000 other fans at Dodger Stadium in Los Angeles, all of us eager to see our idols perform. We held our collective breath while R&B singer Bobby Hebb opened the show with his big hit that year, "Sunny." It was well enough received, but the stadium went crazy as Hebb left the stage, replaced by four energetic Beatles.

At least that's who they seemed to be. From high up in the sold-out stadium where we were sitting, feeling lucky to get tickets at all, the performers below were no more than small dots, ants jumping around on a matchbox stage. Oh well, at least we could enjoy their singing.

But no. Beatlemania had reached such a frenzy we couldn't make out the music at all, not even Ringo's steady beat on the drums. After Bobby Hebb's, the only voices we heard throughout the rest of the concert were those of the afflicted fans around us, shrieking, moaning, sobbing and shouting out their undying devotion to one Beatle or another. It was so frustrating!

It turned out the Beatles themselves agreed with me. They were as frustrated as I was that their concerts had become a cacophony of noise and mayhem. With a track record of hundreds of live shows to their name, they were clearly performers. But above all else The Beatles were brilliant musicians and they wanted their music heard. The performance at Dodger Stadium was on Sunday, August 28. None of us fans knew it then, but the concert the very next evening, at Candlestick Park in San Francisco, would be the last big concert The Beatles ever gave. After August 1966 they went back into the studio, where they could be sure their music would be recorded, and therefore heard.

But The Beatles were more than a performing or a recording rock group. They were an unprecedented force, an icon as a singer-songwriter musical group that many would-be rock stars emulated. All over the country, neighborhood kids were grabbing guitars and drums and harmonicas and practicing together in somebody's garage. Like their idols, most Beatles wannabe groups (and there were plenty) began that way, a few scruffy friends with secondhand instruments, dreaming of making it big.

But there was one big exception. The Monkees!

There was nothing natural or grassroots about the way The Monkees got started. They were pure invention, folks who didn't know each other, answering an ad in a Hollywood trade magazine calling for "Folk & Roll Musicians – Singers for acting roles in new TV series." Out of the hundreds who applied to audition, four were selected and brought together by producers for a 1966 television musical comedy show about the life of a (fake) pop rock group, the premise lifted directly from the movie *A Hard Day's Night.*

An ad for the Monkees auditions

One of those selected to be a Monkee, Davy Jones, may have thought it was fate. Maybe he auditioned remembering how he'd shared the stage a couple of years before with the Beatles themselves, when they appeared on *The Ed Sullivan Show,* although he later revealed that, while he himself was British, he'd actually never heard of The Beatles before that.

Whether fated or not, The Monkees was a complex reflection of the times, a show about a Beatles knock-off group of four mop-tops dressed in double-breasted jackets role-playing a group that wanted to be The Beatles, an imitation of an imitation intended to cash in on the mania. And it came with loads of hype.

The Monkees' debut single was called "Last Train to Clarksville," released a month before the new television show began. The recording was all contrived, the instruments played by an unacknowledged back-up band, the artifice of the group reflected by the fact that only one member of the actual Monkees "group," Mickey Dolenz, was even on the record, on vocals. But it didn't matter. Beatlemania was so powerful it sprinkled popularity like fairy dust over anything that even resembled the Fab Four.

Rock-and-roll station KHJ in Los Angeles, called Boss Radio, got in on the action, sponsoring a contest that summer, for free tickets to Clarksville. "The last train to Clarksville… but where is Clarksville?" the disc jockey teased. "And who wants to get a chance to take the train there and meet The Monkees themselves?"

Listeners were encouraged to call in, every tenth caller a lucky winner who would get to ride the train to meet the new band in Clarksville. By the end of August, 400 teenagers had won and were ready to climb aboard.

Nearly 16, I now had my own room at home, where I kept my plastic AM radio plugged in at my desk, the big round dial faithfully tuned to one of three stations, KRLA, KFWB or KHJ. So of course I heard about the contest. As far as I was concerned, "Last Train to Clarksville" couldn't hold a candle to real Beatles music, but it was catchy enough. My friends and I were looking forward to the new television show, and curious about the contest. Where was the train filled with 400 fans going? As far as we knew, there was no Clarksville in Southern California, with or without a train station.

But that didn't stop the promoters at Boss Radio. No Clarksville? No problem! Just make one up … So they went looking for a town with a train station that was close enough to Los Angeles that the whole event could be accomplished in about 8 hours – from loading 400 teenagers onto the train, and their discovering the mystery location of the fictional Clarksville, to arriving in Clarksville and meeting The Monkees, with time for the train ride back to L. A.

The promoters were pleased when they settled on the place, a pretty seaside village with a vintage train station and, something else needed for the grand scheme, a broad beach. The city leaders even agreed to change the name of the town for a day.

To make it official, the mayor nailed up a temporary sign at the depot: CLARKSVILLE, and at a press conference he handed the band members the keys to the "city." It was a very successful event, with four helicopters landing on the beach, depositing one Monkee apiece, while excited teenagers and curious townspeople gathered to see the performers that the promoters promised were "the next Beatles."

The TV show debuted two nights later and was a huge success, going on to win two Emmys that first season. "Last Train to Clarksville" was number 61 on Billboard's Top 100 List and climbing, soon to be hit #1. In spite of how they got started, The Monkees became tremendously popular. Their records outsold both the Beatles and the Rolling Stones combined in 1967. It was my introduction to the concept of paradox.

In the biography of Monkee Michael Nesmith, a promotion associate at KHJ, Barbara Hamaker, is quoted as saying, "To this day, I don't know how we did it. I was the one who had to type up all the releases and all of the stuff that was involved in getting kids onto the train. ... we used some Podunk town called Del Mar."

And that is how, on September 11, 1966, Del Mar, California got a brand new name.

Chapter 24

Eventide

The day Del Mar became Clarksville was one day after my 16th birthday. I'd love to tell you I was one of those lucky teens welcoming the Monkees to Del Mar, but we weren't even there when the train pulled into the station and the helicopters deposited the four as-yet-unknown pop stars on the sand. The arrival of September in Del Mar always meant it was time for us to return to our house near L. A. so we could get ready for school. So we were already back home when we found out about the event, and even though we never saw The Monkees, we got a big kick out the fact that Clarksville turned out to be Del Mar.

Maybe it was a sign of things to come, because it happened that, in a way, that time in the late 1960s was also the last train to Del Mar... at least for our family. In 1968, after graduating from high school, I worked for my dad's company out of town, living with his youngest sister Shirley and her family during the summer. So I never made it to Del Mar. That fall I left for college, almost a thousand miles away. Two years later my father died in a plane crash. He was alone, flying a small twin-prop plane when it went down in bad weather between Cheyenne and Laramie, in Wyoming. It was Christmas time, just days short of his 46th birthday on December 27. For his wife and kids it was the end of life as we knew it.

Less than a year after Papa's death, Granddaddy died. He was nearly 83, and it may have just been his time. But his retirement from Monolith the year before, after nearly half a century as its president, may have been the last nail in his coffin. Whatever caused it, my grandfather's death was definitely the last nail in the coffin of our family's ownership of La Atalaya.

Grandmother, alone for the first time in more than 60 years, sold the big house at 104 Fremont Place and moved into an apartment with her cook. Concerned about the taxes and upkeep for the run-down Del Mar property, the family decided it too had to be sold. Mama had already sold the house we grew up in, in record time, worried, as was her mother now, about finances. Each of them was learning to be a single woman.

Grandmother died in 1974. She was walking across the living room in her apartment, discussing options for lunch with her cook, when she dropped down dead.

Jessie died too, or in her words, gave up the ghost. That had happened in 1973, after an illness that changed her cozy plump presence into a frail person who seemed, inexplicably, to have become smaller than me. I felt protective of her when we hugged, our roles reversed. I was living in another state and didn't get back to see her at the end.

As a young woman, I tried to reassure myself that this wasn't the essence of adulthood: Everything goes, and everybody dies. I wasn't ready for it. I didn't have enough life behind me to know how ephemeral almost everything is, or to recognize the truth about what lasts.

My grandparents were buried side by side at the original Forest Lawn Memorial Park, as befits owners of mansions of Los Angeles. Forest Lawn, in Glendale, is pure Southern California, large and beautifully groomed, with statuary and wee churches called kirks, and different sections bearing vaguely creepy, amusement-park-like names: Inspiration Slope, Borderland, Dawn of Tomorrow, Vesperland, and sadly, Babyland, shaped like a heart.

The gravesite of Coy and Mildred Burnett is in the section called Eventide. There they will rest eternally alongside celebrities like George Burns and Gracie Allen, Nat King Cole, and Walt Disney. And, across the way is Michael Jackson, residing in his coveted spot in a free-standing, intricately carved marble sarcophagus within the Great Mausoleum, with its Court of Honor, where very special individuals are inducted as "Immortals" by Forest Lawn's Council of Regents.

I attended Grandmother's funeral, held a few days after her death. Compared to the mind-numbing pain of my father's funeral, hers felt right: the honoring of a long full life, peacefully ended. I brought my three-month-old baby, Dorothy Valentine, whose presence cheered everyone up, a reminder of possibilities and the cycle of life.

But there was no funeral for our place in Del Mar. No wake, no service, no rituals of farewell for our family. It was just part of sunny things coming to an end. The place was put up for sale, and we just had to move on.

It was eventide at La Atalaya.

Chapter 25

Uncertain Times

Our family's property in Del Mar didn't sell right away. There was certainly interest early on, but not the kind of interest that could close the deal.

In 2015, nearly 45 years after our family sold La Atalaya, I met Chiquita Abbott, a long-time resident and realtor in Del Mar. The chance to talk with anyone with memories of long-ago Del Mar was not to be missed, so I was excited to meet her.

It turned out Chiquita had a much closer relationship with La Atalaya and our family than I knew. We met at a coffee shop and she arrived carrying a fat, tattered file folder. As she sat down it opened to reveal a bunch of documents that had been jammed in, willy-nilly, over the years, now a mound of letters, legal papers, newspaper clippings, sales brochures for the fabulous "Snakewall Property," and so on, in no particular order.

I suddenly realized that, years after losing my grandparents and my mother, I was meeting a living part of our family history in this person about whom, until that moment, I knew nothing. But then I thought, looking back, the grown-ups never talked about the details of selling our place in Del Mar. For us kids, our special place just disappeared, never to be discussed again. Unspeakable.

But now I was the grown-up, and Chiquita was more than willing to talk. She told me she was involved in early efforts to buy the run-down property. She started looking for a particular document, and apologized for the disorganized file, adding "I don't throw much out."

That turned out to be a bonus. There, among the other documents, I caught sight of a handwritten letter, and I pulled it out, thinking "I know that handwriting!" Sure enough, it was my aunt King's distinctive bold cursive. In the letter she identified herself as Kingsbury Burnett, Executrix of the property. It was dated May, 1972.

Chiquita said that back then she was in touch with both of my mother's sisters. In the spring after Granddaddy died, my aunt Anne contacted Chiquita's real estate firm. Sure enough, there was a letter in the folder from Anne claiming to "represent Mrs. Burnett in considering the sale of her Del Mar property," and asking if there would be any interest in seeing it. Anne was surely worried about finances now that Granddaddy was dead, as she had relied on his support for many years.

Quite soon, Chiquita had clients interested in the property, seeing it as a development opportunity, but done "properly," she reassured me, "with low density." After several conversations with Anne the realtor learned that it was actually her sister Kingsbury who was officially handling things. Chiquita contacted King, hoping to get in early, before anyone else could grab the place up. She offered $300,000 on behalf of her clients, and included as earnest money a check for one thousand dollars, in the hope of sealing the deal.

A copy of the letter was right there in the file, equal parts reassurance and urgency. "We envision the land carrying only first class structures. With the use of an excellent land planner, the large stands of Torrey pines will remain, and the rugged cliffs left mostly intact." This was followed by a round of questions about how quickly the sale might be completed, and several suggestions for cutting corners to speed things along, while avoiding paying various taxes. All above board, of course. The letter concluded with a soothing message.

Chiquita and her clients could have saved themselves the trouble. King's letter, in response to the offer, clarified in no uncertain terms that the property, as part of the assets of Coy Burnett's estate, was in probate and under the jurisdiction of the California courts. Chiquita Abbott was thanked and her check was returned. It was there in the disorganized file folder 45 years later, a little the worse for wear: $1,000, made out to Kingsbury Burnett.

It was a setback, but Chiquita didn't lose interest. Probate would end at some point. By August, 1972 she had put together a different team of firms interested in "the development and marketing of that some twenty acres 'behind the wall' in Del Mar." But that also failed to go through.

Things dragged on at La Atalaya. It's unclear whether there was a temporary owner of the property during the mid-'70s, like a bank, or if my grandfather's probate dragged on as well, while Chiquita and other realtors looked to make a sweet deal. In any case, in 1977, after many false starts and surely as many false hopes on my family's part, there was finally a buyer for the property.

And what a buyer he turned out to be.

Chapter 26

The Mysterious Mr. Smith

In the early 1980s I flew into LAX, the international airport in L. A., with Bruce, the man who would one day become my husband. We stayed a few days in Marina Del Rey with my mother, before heading south to visit friends who had moved to San Diego.

It went without saying that, since we were going in that direction, we would take a slight detour off the interstate to drive into Del Mar and up the winding roads, Seaview and Zapo, that led toward the gate of our grandparents' old property. Not the main gate with the beautiful arch at the top of the hill, where Serpentine Drive circled around. No, it was the gate on the east slope of the property, off Gatun Street, that pulled me, the gate we had transited so many times each August as children.

It was more than a decade since our family had vacationed at La Atalaya, but my heart didn't seem to know. It gave the same leap it always had as we made that last sharp turn in the road and the gates came into view. I was right back in those magical first moments that happened early every August. They began when we turned off the highway onto Seaview and proceeded to snake our way up to the top of the ridge, all of us kids bouncing a little in our seats, as if to make the car go faster. Cresting the hill, we could see east to the river valley below us, and then, finally, rounding the bend, there was the wall, with its gates open wide to greet us. "Come on in," they always seemed to say. "It's great to see you kids again!"

Only this time the gates that had welcomed us each summer were closed. As we pulled up and Bruce stopped the car, we could see they were not just closed, they were secured with an impressively heavy chain, from which hung a massive padlock. The lack of a welcome could not have been plainer.

On the side of the gate there was a button, like a doorbell. So I pushed it, a little timidly, suspecting it might not work.

But it did. Below us, on the other side of the wall, we heard a door slam and through the wrought iron gate soon glimpsed a man walking slowly up the driveway. He was accompanied by two dogs, large muscular Dobermans, one on each side, straining on their short leather leashes. They looked trained to kill. So did the man. As he got closer, we could see the bulge at the guy's waist, the handle of a pistol casually visible. And when he began to speak we could see his broken and missing teeth. Those teeth completed the image of a gangster's henchman.

"Yeah? Can I help you?" He stood a few feet back from the gate and made no move to open it, not appearing the least bit interested in helping us. The dogs froze beside him and stared at us through squinty yellow eyes, like they were hoping for a chance to attack.

Make our day…

"Um, hi. My name is Brier and my grandparents owned this property for a long time, I used to come here with my family every summer…" I stammered, lamely ending with, "…the Burnetts…? Coy Burnett?"

The man with bad teeth stared at me dully, giving no sign that he knew or cared who Coy Burnett might be.

I persisted a little weakly, "We were just here from out of town and, uh, I just wondered if we could walk around just a little, you know, so I could show my friend where I used to come as a kid…"

Apparently the man with the dogs had tired of our conversation. He hitched up his pants a little, causing me to glance involuntarily at the glint of metal in his waistband, and then he got quickly to the point:

"Well, that would be up to Mr. Smith. And Mr. Smith isn't here."

With that he turned and walked back down the driveway. I hadn't noticed before that he had a slight limp.

Bruce and I exchanged glances. Mr. Smith??? Yeah, right. The gangster image was now complete.

I later learned from my sister, Claire, that she and her friend Cindy had made a similar pilgrimage to the property, a couple of years before Bruce and I were turned away. But that time the owner was at home.

And it turned out his name really *was* Smith!

Still, Claire's story didn't make me sorry we'd missed him, even though I envied her the chance to see the property. Mr. Smith had apparently been quite happy to open the gates to the two attractive young women standing there, one explaining she was related to the former owners. They followed him down the driveway to the door of the main house, where he asked them to wait just a moment. He emerged a couple of minutes later, the legs of his shorts rolled up like tight-fitting swim trunks, his shirt half unbuttoned. His explanation, that it was getting hot, did nothing to calm the flutter growing in Claire's stomach.

"Come this way, I'll show you how I've fixed up the old chicken house." As he turned to lead the way, the smell of stale liquor lingered in the air.

Looking at one another for reassurance – strength in numbers and all that – Claire and Cindy followed Mr. Smith a little more slowly, trying to avoid glimpsing his skimpily clad butt as they figured out how to leave as quickly as possible.

Inside the old concrete building Mr. Smith bragged about having the walls painted and all the other improvements he'd made. Then he opened a door in the floor that led downstairs, into the root cellar where bootleg liquor had been stored decades before.

"Come see what I've done with my wine cellar." He started down the stairs, looking back at the young women. It was less a request than a demand that they follow. Again they reluctantly complied.

Four steps down Claire had seen enough. Red carpet. Red flocked wallpaper, or was that actually red carpet on the walls? A daybed, or maybe just a bed, up against one wall. A bed in a wine cellar? There was no sign of shelves for wine. No wine, not a bottle in sight.

"Maybe he drank it all," she was thinking as she tried to figure out how she and Cindy could make a polite getaway.

"What are you waiting for?" Mr. Smith had turned to look up the stairs, his face a little contorted with a sneer he perhaps intended to be a reassuring smile.

"We've got to go." Claire turned to Cindy, who bolted up the steps, Claire right behind. "Thanks for the tour," they called, belatedly remembering their manners. They ran all the way to the gate and gratefully through it, where they jumped into their car, caught their breath and fled.

Claire's description years later made us laugh, but our giggles didn't completely mask the creepiness of the whole thing. "You should have smelled his breath. Or seen the look on Cindy's face when he came out wearing those rolled up shorts. But that so-called wine cellar..." Claire shook her head, as if to erase the memory. "I'm not kidding – it was a place you'd keep a sex slave."

Actually, James E. Smith had a thing for beds. There's no evidence he kept sex slaves, but his penchant for beds is a matter of record. In 1978 Gregory Dennis of the *Del Mar Surfcomber* newspaper had an interesting story to report, about the new owner of the "mysterious Snakewall property" and his run-in with the fire department. And it all started with beds...

Mr. Smith, along with being reclusive and a bit of a mystery to the local folks, was allegedly a businessman of great wealth, and among his assets was a convalescent home near Los Angeles that was being updated. After purchasing La Atalaya in the late 1970s, Smith had a number of old hospital beds shipped south from the nursing home to his new property in Del Mar. The dilapidated mattresses in their rusting frames were scattered along the ridge among the Torrey pines looking out over the ocean. He told the reporter he used them as chaise lounges, handy for spontaneous sunbathing, with a view.

The local fire department got involved when someone called in an alarm, reporting thick smoke rising from their new neighbor's property, probably identifying it as the Snakewall Property. Perhaps remembering stories of the terrible house fire up there years before, the firefighters raced up the winding streets to the top of the hill, to Serpentine Drive, where they jumped out of the truck and prepared to save the day.

They could smell burning and see thick smoke, but the gate was padlocked. They started to cut the chain so they could get inside and save the day. But instead of a grateful welcome, they were greeted by the new owner running toward them, waving a pistol. The firefighters jumped into the fire truck and hastened back down the hill, no doubt sharing some choice words about this new resident of Del Mar.

Talking to the reporter, Smith insisted that there was no need for the fire department to get involved. He was simply burning old mattresses in the swimming pool, no problem as far as he was concerned.

That wasn't the end of it. According to the report in the *Surfcomber*, the story about Mr. Smith had some interesting twists: "The mattress burning isn't the only strange incident in which Smith has lately been involved... on the day he was initially scheduled to appear on the charges arising from the burning... he instead cruised the parking lot of the Vista courthouse in his Cadillac limo, dressed only in a jock strap and with flowers and the barrels of two rifles sticking out of the sun roof."

Noting that others in town, observers of these recent incidents, described the newest resident of Del Mar as "having a screw loose somewhere," Gregory Dennis asked Smith if he considered himself to be eccentric. Upon reflection, Mr. Smith said no. The reporter challenged this, wondering how many other Del Mar residents would go out on their property and light a bunch of old mattresses on fire. According to Dennis, Smith's reply came quickly:

"Yes – but how many other Del Mar residents own the Snakewall?"

Chapter 27

Snakebit!

Things grew quiet again at La Atalaya, once the burning mattresses and flashy limo rides got sorted out. Beyond the newspaper coverage of his run-ins with the police, there would be no record of the early years Mr. Smith spent at my grandparents' former estate if it weren't for a surfer's blog.

As a teenager the blogger apparently lived next door to La Atalaya, and wrote fondly about the early 1980s in Del Mar. Reminiscing about the great surfing, he also recounted stories about his weird neighbors at the Snakewall place and how he planted marijuana inside their property. He could climb over the wall and walk around whenever he wanted, unless the owners' Doberman Pinschers showed up and chased him back over it.

For a while – aside from pot plants and suspicious guard dogs – there was no more excitement at La Atalaya. And it might have stayed quiet, but James Smith wasn't just sunbathing up there on the hill. He was hatching new plans for his unique property, way beyond a handy place to discard hospital beds. Most of his schemes seemed to center on making a lot of money. Over the years Smith proposed selling the property to the city for various purposes. There was a standing offer to sell to anyone willing to pay a cool $21 million. He claimed that he came up with this astronomical figure by adding four zeros to the address, 2100 Gatun Street.

Ultimately the grandest vision won out: a luxury resort with a "world-class, five star" 500-room hotel the likes of which Del Mar had never seen, at least according to Smith's final proposal to the Del Mar City Council. But the Council had different ideas, and Mr. Smith faced an uphill battle. The Del Mar City Planners were not keen on a big development, and recommended preserving the property at the top of the ridge, with its mostly wild acreage and rare Torrey pines, for a nature park or similar function.

Smith countered with the claim that a luxury resort would bring a million dollars yearly revenue into the community, minimally, and proposed a citywide nonbinding vote on the issue, a longstanding tradition in Del Mar. He was so convinced the residents would express unbridled enthusiasm for his proposal that he offered to pay all the costs of the special election himself. Finally, in the mid-1980s, Smith and his minions had gathered enough signatures to force the City Council to hold a special vote. Measure C would put the development of a hotel resort on my grandparents' old property before the citizens of Del Mar.

In anticipation, Smith distributed colorful brochures filled with glossy photographs and glowing phrases about his proposal, entitled "Facts You Should Know About the Snakewall Property in Del Mar." It began by calling attention, accurately, to the historic significance that a hotel had played in much of Del Mar's past. From there, the "facts" became more like promises: claims of money that would pour into the city as well as the numerous benefits to the voters, including half-price use of the resort facilities for all residents, not to mention putting the city on the map at a whole new level. "Architects from all over the world will be invited to submit their designs for consideration ... the result will be a landmark structure for Del Mar and a fitting enhancement of the Snakewall Property."

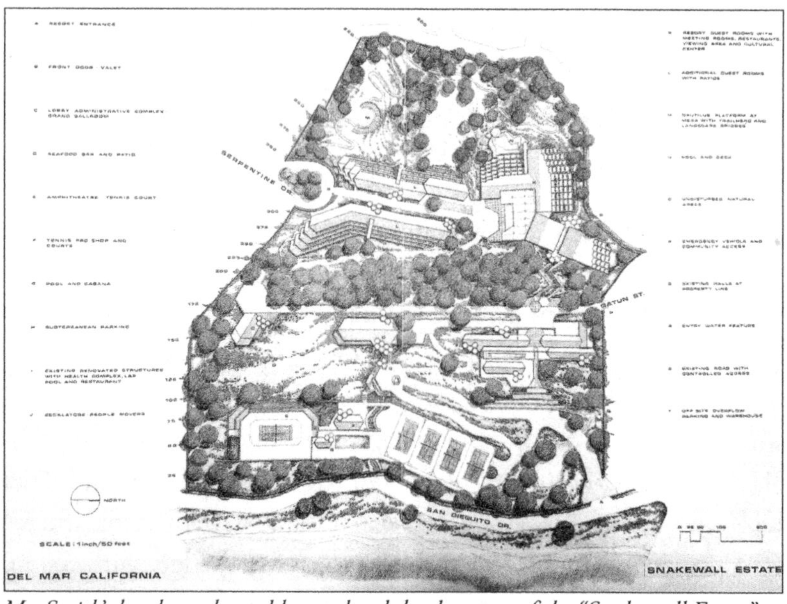

Mr. Smith's brochure showed how a hotel development of the "Snakewall Estate" would fit into the community.

There was even an election slogan:

IF YOU AGREE
WITH WHAT YOU SEE
VOTE YES ON MEASURE C

Smith had a lot riding on the vote, and as incentive to the good folks of Del Mar, the ballot proposal promised to give the City of Del Mar "all proceeds in excess of $9 million" from the sale of the 20-acre estate to a developer if voters approved a change in zoning that would allow for the construction of a hotel on the property. However, as a disincentive, Smith announced publicly that, if the initiative measure lost at the polls, he planned to sell off the estate for 20 one-acre house sites.

When a reporter asked him what he would do if the vote didn't go his way, Smith responded: "If I had half the money that William Randolph Hearst had, or even 1% of it, I might just build up the wall to 12 feet or so and say to hell with the rest of Del Mar, but I would rather open up the property and invite everyone in."

James Smith didn't make a lot of friends during his years in Del Mar. Maybe his inflammatory words, crazy antics and habit of conflicting with anybody who saw things differently were ultimately Smith's undoing.

In any case, he never pulled off the financial coup he'd hoped for. Measure C was defeated. And, in spite of some temporary success that allowed for a part of the wall to be cut away to build a couple of homes, in the end the Council and the citizens of Del Mar won, and the large estate was once again deemed to be a single property.

Now James E. Smith had a huge white elephant on his hands. Deciding enough was enough, Mr. Smith put the Snakewall Property up for sale, crossing his fingers and asking for $7.5 million. This was almost 10 times what he'd paid, in spite of the fact that the actual property was now smaller, as some of the original acreage had been sold off.

The *Los Angeles Times* ran a story about Smith in 1991. The headline could be his epitaph as far as Del Mar goes: "Snakewall Owner Is Snakebit by Del Mar Politics."

Chapter 28

Rescued

It isn't easy, selling a white elephant, especially one that costs millions of dollars. The property sat. Mr. Smith, entangled as he was in feuds with his neighbors and notices of violations of one kind and another, dropped the initial price by 40 percent. Still no one showed an interest in buying his property. No surprise. The once-beautiful estate was massively overgrown, neglected and littered with trash and rusting hospital beds.

Rule #1 in selling a white elephant: Never call it a white elephant. The advertisements for the sale of La Atalaya certainly did not. They were, in fact, downright lyrical, and didn't mention anything at all about a snake wall.

> **SAN DIEGO COUNTY'S LARGEST COASTAL ESTATE: A Del Mar, California Landmark**
>
> **15 ACRES ON TOP OF THE WORLD:** This historic, 15-acre Torrey Pines Paradise soars above the Pacific Ocean. Unobstructable whitewater, back country, city and mountain views can be seen from every vantage point… the unmatched privacy of this walled, gated compound offers an overwhelming setting of seclusion, security and serenity.

Flowery language aside, the property was indeed a landmark, and even bigger than the advertisement proclaimed. Full of the history of Del Mar, and with a compelling history of its own, the property's attributes could not be ignored indefinitely. La Atalaya was patient, waiting for someone who could see past the ruins and debris, to discover her windswept magnificence.

Eventually the property sold. Roughly 100 tons of vegetation, rusted metal and other debris had to be cleared away. A crew worked to restore and strengthen the wall. When it came to the original garage-stalls-turned-bunkrooms, it turned out that remodeling was not an option. They were constructed not just with concrete, but with concrete poured around steel I-beams, forming columns integral to the buildings. So the old place was completely torn down – there may have been some explosives involved – and rebuilt, as faithfully as possible, to Requa's original design.

La Atalaya began to shine again, proud of her natural beauty and her history.

The Family Historian

When it came to family history, there was no one better to ask than Kingsbury Burnett Gooding. Not only was she the eldest child of Coy and Mildred Burnett, but King lived at home well into her adulthood before she married late and had her two sons, Neal and Owen. She worked at Monolith for years as well, and was close to both of her parents. Devoted to family, and the oldest living member of the Burnett clan, my aunt King was the keeper of the family stories. I "interviewed" her once about her days growing up at La Atalaya.

Reflecting on those long-ago days, King seemed to slip into the past. "Beyond the drying yard and the chicken coops, the road turned. There were several papaya plants and at least eight avocado trees." Kingsbury closed her eyes, the better to see it all. "At the bend in the road there was a mulberry bush growing over a large trellis. Down the hill below the outbuildings, there was a level of citrus trees, and below them the flatter ground at the bottom held large vegetable gardens, with a row of Tamarack trees for a wind break. There was an orchard with grapes, apricots and elephant heart plums, and rows of corn off in another section."

She remembered the animals that lived alongside them on the property in the '20s and '30s, the horses and dogs, the goats raised for milk, the chickens, ducks and pigeons raised for eating. And, of course, eggs. "The family ate lots of eggs," she recalled, "and we had fried chicken every Sunday, along with lettuce wedges, hot biscuits and freshly pressed grape juice."

Chapter 29

The Second Architect

A new house now stands on the rocky ridge at the top of the property at La Atalaya. It was designed by celebrated Mexico City architect Alberto Kalach, who produced a fantastic modernist structure that appears to grow out of the ridge and stretch toward the sea and the setting sun.

Alberto Kalach is an interesting contrast to Coy Burnett's original architect. Richard Requa from the Midwest built in a Mediterranean-Mexican style, while Kalach employed natural materials and minimalism, widely used in modern Mexican architecture. This includes the modernist use of concrete, the defining construction material for the newest house at La Atalaya, a fact that surely would have pleased my grandfather.

Kalach studied architecture at the Universidad Iberoamericana, Mexico City, and completed graduate studies later at Cornell University in New York. In 1981 he cofounded the firm "Taller de Arquitectura X," and in the early 2000s Kalach began to focus on the urban planning problems of his gigantic hometown of Mexico City. As part of the ambitious plan México: Ciudad Futura ("Future City"), his work has included a lakes project to deal with the city's existing water problems, called Recovering the City of Lakes. Kalach's influence has been widespread. When asked to identify a great work of modern architecture in Mexico, many point to Biblioteca Vasconcelos, Kalach's soaring library of glass in Mexico City.

Kalach's vision for La Atalaya was a house in harmony with the setting, with its protruding rocks and craggy slopes, a house built without destroying the integrity and natural beauty of the land. When the building was completed in late 2008, a release from the architectural firm described the project:

> "... Inserted on the top of a narrow ridge, the house overlooks the Pacific Ocean, the valleys, and the distant mountains. A 360-degree view to enjoy the horizon, the sunrise and the sunset. The distant rumor of the town and highway is filtered through the slope of woods that surrounds the place."

With the building of the new house, the charred patio and crumbled chimney of our childhood memories, the ruins that had survived for over 60 years and so long served as a reminder of times gone by, were demolished. The groundbreaking eliminated, finally, all traces of my mother's childhood home.

A Flashback

When the new house at La Atalaya was about to be built, our family was invited to the groundbreaking party. I was excited to go. We got a tour of the property, and shared our family history. We got to see the plans for the new house, and the big landscape map from the 1920s.

As everyone admired Kalach's model for what is now a fabulous home of concrete, wood and glass overlooking the Pacific, I had a flash from the past: my sister and me playing Anne Frank. I overheard a conversation about turning the old chicken house into a guest cottage and found myself bitten with a memory, the sharp smell of chlorine. It was the August after I'd read *Diary of a Young Girl*, when Claire and I played endless variations of hiding from the Nazis in the old chicken house. At some point we came up with the plan - she insists it was all my idea - to take a bucket of bleach and scrub the mildew off the upstairs walls (remember, everything was concrete). One afternoon, while scrubbing away diligently (and surely killing young brain cells), we were startled by a sudden movement in the corner of the room.

Before we could even register it enough to react, our cat Fluffy sprinted across the room, leapt in the air and caught a bat that had flown too low. Starting with the tail, she then proceeded to eat it as its wings flapped in vain, and Claire and I sat stunned, all in a haze of chlorine fumes.

That's surely how it is for many people whose families had wealth or fame or celebrity at some point and then things changed. While the outside world conjures up glamorous images embellished by unlikely legends and boundless imagination, we too remember the good times, but also the mildew, the rattlesnakes and the dismembered bats.

Chapter 30
The Wall, Part Three

While much has changed at La Atalaya, the wall is still there. Worn and wounded by the passage of time, breached in a couple of places by the encroachment of development, it's now refurbished and holding strong, proud of its history and its heritage.

If I could interview the wall, I would ask it about those long-ago times of plenty when it enclosed the beautifully landscaped estate, and about how it protected the family in the hard times. I'd inquire whether it remembers every person who has come through its gates, and I'd ask what it was like the day of the fire.

I'm positive the wall would say its favorite memories are those times it was walked upon, generations of young bare feet (and lightly clad bottoms) scooting and scampering up and down the hill on its capable spine. I imagine it would tell me a bit wistfully that now the only ones who walk its length are those employed to inspect and maintain it, preserving its historical significance. I'd ask the wall if it misses children's feet, and if it's proud to be a treasured antique.

I'd want to inquire whether the wall remembers its beginnings, when a crew of men from Mexico arrived with picks and shovels and wooden frames into which enormous amounts of concrete would be poured. I'd ask if it can recall the youngest man on the job, a boy really, only 16 years old, named Nick Esparza. It was his job to walk up ahead of the rest of the crew who were doing the actual construction of the wall, carrying a shovel for digging holes for the concrete columns to be poured. In his other hand he carried a long stick, which he used to poke the underbrush as he went along, and then the shovel served another purpose (with any luck): beheading the rattlesnakes that lurked there.

I don't know if the wall remembers the boy, but the man who was that 16-year-old never forgot the wall, telling stories about those long-ago days walking up and down steep rocky hills, about that shovel and those rattlers.

I'd tell the wall about the big old landscape map signed by Richard Requa, found during the restoration, rolled up and forgotten, with its meticulous plans for the trees and plantings, the skeet-shooting range and the stables, the gates and the wall itself.

I'd show the old photos, and we'd reminisce about all the lives touched by this unique place, from Caroline Schafer and her husband discovering the location on top of the ridge to the workers who built the wall; from the groundskeeper whose still blew up above the garages during Prohibition to the soldiers stationed on the hillside in World War II; from Jessie raising Val during the 1930s to her returning with Val's kids in the 1950s. All here for a while.

I'd be curious if the wall preferred the elegant early days, with the shadowy lath house filled with orchids, or those rough and ready mid-century years when we kids played jail in there, stepping among the shards of broken flower pots. I'd wonder what it's been like, witnessing the transformations over the years, and we'd metaphorically shake our heads over the James Smith era. Of course we'd share a moment of solidarity in our distaste for the misnomer "snakewall."

And I'd get a big kick out of telling the story of an unusual discovery. It was on the lower concrete wall in the lath house, written in a young boy's hand, faded over the decades but still legible. We'd agree, the wall and I, that King would be pleased her younger son had left his mark on the property:

I OWEN OF ENCINO DO HEREBY CURSE THIS TUNNEL

* * *

La Atalaya in my grandparents' day was a flourishing estate and working farm. During my childhood the gardens had disappeared, replaced with nothing but coarse sand, and over time large parts of the property became a no man's land filled with sand burrs, cactus and rattlesnakes. When we visited as kids, any paths that had once been there were long overgrown or invisible. Then in Mr. Smith's day, the overgrowth burgeoned, sharing the space with metal debris and decomposing mattresses.

Now, as La Atalaya approaches her century mark, the land is being cared for again. Through the stewardship of the current owners, hundreds of olive trees have been planted, along with plums, citrus and pomegranate trees, avocados and several varieties of palms. And they have been warmly welcomed, as we've all been, by the native Torrey pines, the oldest inhabitants of this special place.

Olive trees provide shade, and support the Mediterranean character of La Atalaya.

Epilogue, 1994

Of the Sea, Part Two

It was many years after our family sold the "Snakewall Property" that my mother Valentine, the main star of the fanciful legend about the property's name, was dying of cancer. A longtime family friend, John Ballinger, had for months been trying to persuade her to come for a visit to his vacation home on the coast of Maui, a place she loved, and she finally agreed. Since she was quite weak by then, I travelled with her on the long flight, across the Pacific to paradise.

We stepped off the plane into warm, moist air smelling of tropical flowers and the ocean. Soon we were bowing our heads to receive the fragrant leis draped around our necks in welcome. Aloha.

John had placed his old friend Val in the master bedroom with its sliding glass doors that opened onto a small deck overlooking the water and the sound of waves crashing rhythmically on the rocky shoreline below. Mama spent much of that visit in bed, with the doors wide open, listening, gazing out at the sky, or with her eyes closed, looking peaceful.

Just a few days into our trip she stopped being able to walk. It turned out she had developed spinal tumors, but we didn't know that then. What we did know was that we had to cross personal boundaries like never before. I found myself in a reversed role, as happens, helping her get on the toilet or into the shower, drying her off. Caring for her. I had never seen my private, proper mother naked before.

We stayed for nine days, and had some good meals together in her room. She told a few stories, when she had the energy, including her memories of summers as a girl on Catalina Island. She remembered playing with the Mexican and Indian kids, the excited mothers chaperoning, the flying fish, the canvas tents and big dining hall where they all ate together.

We talked about other times on the island, when she and Papa took us kids there in the '50s, when she took my young family, and then her grandsons there in the '90s, to a much fancier Avalon than the rustic tent village she remembered. We talked about how much things change.

The last day on Maui, Mama let John and me hoist her out of her bed and into an overstuffed armchair in the living room where she and I watched the movie *Free Willy*, about a boy and a whale. It was when the boy was struggling to release Willy, the captive whale, back into the wild that my mother, one of the least sentimental people I've ever known, was able to weep. Her gray blue eyes filled and ran over with tears as Willy broke loose and escaped into the freedom of the sea.

"I'm not sure I'll ever get off this island," she said quietly as the movie credits were running. I couldn't tell if that was her fear or her wish.

The next morning it did come time to leave Maui, and it was indeed touch and go whether we'd be able to get her onto the plane back to California. John and I had just learned that it had to be pre-arranged for someone to fly who couldn't walk on their own. Having not made such pre-arrangements, we were worried we couldn't disguise the fact of her immobility. But between us we maneuvered her on, with Mama helping as she could, mostly by smiling and nodding pleasantly. Maybe people thought she was tipsy, but it worked. I settled back into the comfortable first-class seat with relief, knowing friends would meet us at LAX with a wheelchair.

As John said goodbye, he took me aside. "I'm sorry this trip was so hard on your mom. I feel bad she was stuck in bed, with nothing to do."

"You know, I think the waves were the best part of this trip for her. The sound of them outside her bedroom, she said she liked lying there surrounded by the smells and sounds she grew up with.... She had the ocean. I think it's helping her let go."

Mama made it back home to her condo that first night we got to the mainland. But she was hospitalized the next day. Then it had been a long journey, from hospital to nine wretched days in the nursing home and now, back to the hospital, in a room in a former pediatrics wing.

It was there, surrounded by Minnie and Mickey in old-fashioned bathing suits, that I asked my mother about her wishes.

"I know you want to be cremated. But I wondered... what do you want us to do with the ashes?"

I felt protective of her. No one should have to have this talk, and we all need to. My mother seemed to take it in stride. She didn't need protection.

"Well, I hadn't really thought about that." Subdued by pain and morphine, she seemed to float, observing the rest of us peacefully from someplace else. "It's really up to you kids. I just want to be in a beautiful place."

She never got to go back home, and died three weeks after we returned from Maui. Her death taught me the only prayer to offer toward any person facing this greatest of transitions: May they go in peace. My mother's peace came in the form of a rich, full life and, when it came to the end, being able to ask me to stay in the hospital room with her, joking around with family and friends even on the last day of her life, holding my sister's hand, slipping into a coma and then gently into death.

She died on June 26th. Later that summer Claire and Patrick and I with our families went to Catalina Island, where on a perfect August day, we rented two aluminum fishing boats and motored around the island to an empty bay. There we lost ourselves in play and water and memories. We'd stopped at a deli and, on the cleanest beach towel available, served sandwiches and chips and fruit. We built sandcastles and dug holes, played poison waves and went body surfing (and no one wiped out). It was a calm surf, actually, and the gentleness of the waves and wet sand, the cooling breezes and blue sky made us forget that the sun was beating down on us full force. I think we were kids again, that afternoon, back at the 16th Street Beach in Del Mar, relaxed, carefree..., and we completely forgot about sunblock. We would all pay the price that night and during the rest of the trip, as we tried to soothe our bright red skin. But the relaxation and affection were worth it.

As the sun began to head toward the horizon, we knew it was almost time to say goodbye to the little bay. We gathered up our things and got into the boats and went out into the water, where we scattered Mama's remains into the great Pacific Ocean.

Each of us, starting with me, as the oldest child, and ending with Nick and then Masami, as the youngest grandchildren, reached into the container of ashes and grabbed a small gritty handful which we then threw into the water. The sunlight caused the minerals in the bone fragments to sparkle for a moment before they sank heavily from view. Claire had brought a bouquet of ten daisies; after our handful of ashes, we each threw a flower into the water, in remembrance.

Five-year-old Sami threw in her little handful, and then tossed out the last daisy. As we all watched it slowly drift to join the other flowers, there was movement under the surface of the water. We all fell back as a dolphin burst up through the surface, right through the floating petals, smiling sweetly as only a dolphin can do.

We all knew it was Mama, saying goodbye. She had made it home.

The wide blue ocean, like the wall at La Atalaya, was a great teacher. The wall taught us about perspective and connections. The ocean taught us about the beauty of impermanence, while it invited us to appreciate the everlasting, deeper rhythms of life, and the faithful presence of the sea and the land.

Afterword

Walking Walls

I have been walking the wall all my life. As children we were doing it and as an adult I have been remembering it, writing about it, even researching it. Reflecting. We all walk walls. Straddle differences that we encounter in our lives.

It was walking the wall at Del Mar that introduced me to the complexities and contradictions of our lives. While my mother and her brother, Coy Jr., would have had a lovely estate inside the walls, complete with avocado trees and citrus groves and a stable, by the time my siblings and I walked the wall in the middle of the 20th century it was a different story. On one side of the wall was iceplant, succulent and squishy, with long-lasting flowers in coral and pink and fiery orange that lit up the hillsides with their tropical bloom. On the other side it was mostly sand burrs, tumbleweeds and scraggly cactus.

It should have been easy to decide which way to fall if we had to, but that's where the paradox came in. While we would prefer a gentle, albeit moist, landing on iceplant, we also wanted to fall inside, on our own property, the side full of burrs.

While walls tend to represent enclosure, constraint and separation, for us the wall meant freedom, abandon and togetherness. Our wall, with its strange myths and legends as the Snake Wall, may have kept some snakes out. But it kept a lot in too. It wasn't simple. There was no single truth.

We tend to experience walls from the bottom, or the side. Walking along the top of the wall as it slithered and slid up and down hills taught us to see things in a different way. From up on top, walls seem to connect more than they divide. Too often we have a ceiling, literal or figurative, plaster or glass, that prevents us from standing on top. Walking the wall taught us about perspective.

A wall marks an intersection, a meeting place, connecting one side with the other even as it separates them.

We have become accustomed to the concept of interpersonal boundaries. It's common in therapy, or you may have encountered it if you watched *Oprah*, to speak about "good" and "bad" boundaries in describing our relationships with one another, as if this distinction is just common sense.

And yet...what is a boundary? It can be a prison wall, thick and windowless, complete with barbed wire and broken glass. Yet just as likely, as between states or countries, a boundary can be as fluid as a river or as imaginary as a line that ebbs and flows with the whimsy of politics or the spoils of war.

A boundary is a meeting place, an intersection of differences, and it is only in looking back at walking the wall that I discover the many intersections that shaped my family's life at Del Mar: Grown-up and child. Black and brown and white. Rich and poor. Slough and sea. Servant and landowner. The Turf Club and the Blue Room. Upstairs and downstairs. Present ... and past.

We all walk walls. They run around and through and between our lives, inside and out, connecting us even as they mark our differences.

We all walk walls. Too often we scurry along the base, frantic and fearing what might be on the other side. But the view from up on top of a wall can be amazing: the freedom to recognize that we're all connected.

A view of the wall at La Atalaya, still standing

Acknowledgments

I am grateful to so many for helping create this book:

- To my grandparents for finding and sharing the property on the hill in Del Mar.
- To my daughter Eleanor Miller whose research and writing about her grandmother – my mother, Valentine – inspired me to write about her too.
- To Roxanne Sadovsky, who has helped me learn to write with my heart and my gut as well as my head, and to our writing group where that happens.
- To Larry Brooks, president of the Del Mar Historical Society, for his enthusiastic encouragement and knowledgeable fact-checking.
- To longtime Del Mar residents Hortensia Moriel Trejo, Don Terwilliger, Chiquita Abbott and Margaret McIntosh, whose memories helped fill in the gaps.
- To Ron and Lucille Neeley for inviting me into their amazing home and for sharing in the love of the place.
- To my daughter Dorothy Miller, my sister Claire Kiyono, my aunts Lois Scott and Shirley (Ann) Yarbrough, and my good friends Heidi Carlson, Ginny D'Angelo, Cathy Roberts, Nancy Dawn Van Beest and Bob Wold, for reading the manuscript and giving such helpful feedback.
- To my husband Bruce Minor, who listened patiently while I read it aloud, cover to cover, on my 68th birthday.
- To the many amazing families whom I have had the honor of knowing during my years as a family therapist, for teaching me that every family's story is important and worth telling.
- To Linnea Dayton, whose knowledge and creativity, thoughtful editing and generosity of time and energy in publishing this book, have helped make the experience more than I could have ever hoped for.
- And, finally, to my aunt Kingsbury, the keeper of the family stories, not to mention old letters, photos and documents. I could not have written this book without you, King.

References

Introduction: Walking the Wall

"Chronology of the Indigenous Peoples of San Diego County." Compiled by Nancy Carol Carter, University of San Diego School of Law, University of San Diego, **www.sandiego.edu/native-american/chronology/**

1 How It All Started

Ancestry.com / Birth, marriage, military and DMV records

Autobiographical papers of Coy Burnett, date unknown

Autobiographical papers of Mildred Kingsbury Burnett, date unknown

2 The City of Angels

Gracey, Pat. "The Scar on the Mountain: The Spirit of Tehachapi." *The Loop*, 28 Oct. 2017, **www.theloopnewspaper.com/story/2017/10/28/ community/the-scar-on-the-mountain/3962.html**

Hammond, Jon. "Jon Hammond: 100 Years of History Written in Cement at Monolith/Lehigh Southwest." *Tehachapi News,* 1 Sept. 2016, **www.tehachapinews.com/lifestyle/2009/05/27/jon-hammond-100-years-of-history-written-in-cement-at-monolith-lehigh-southwest.html**

"History." Mission Basilica San Diego de Alcalá, 1 Sept. 2016, **www.missionsandiego.org/visit/history/**

Johnson, Joan. "Mural Honors Vital Part of Tehachapi's History: Coy Burnett – The Man Behind The Name." Angelfire, *The Tehachapi News*, 23 June 2008, **www.angelfire.com/sd/thswarriors/news56.html**

Jones, Glenn. "The Portland Cement Factory at Monolith, California." *The Fahey Files – John Fahey – The Portland Cement Factory at Monolith, California*, Aug. 1998, **www.johnfahey.com/pages/portland.html**

Pool, Bob. "City of Angels' First Name Still Bedevils Historians." *Los Angeles Times,* 26 Mar. 2005, **www.latimes.com/archives/la-xpm-2005-mar-26-me-name26-story.html**

"Pueblo de Los Ángeles." *Wikipedia,* Wikimedia Foundation, 1 Nov. 2020, **en.wikipedia.org/wiki/Pueblo_de_Los_Angeles**

3 Portland Cement – and Potash

"A Brief History of the Danish West Indies." *Virgin Islands History*, **www.virgin-islands-history.dk/eng/vi_hist.asp**

Kosmatka, Steven H. and Michelle L. Wilson, "Introduction to Concrete." *Design and Control of Concrete Mixtures, 16th ed.*, Portland Cement Association, 2016, pp. 1–16, **members.cement.org/EBiz55/Bookstore/EB001.16-Ch.1-Intro-to-Concrete-LR.pdf**

"Monolith Historical Marker." The Historical Marker Database, 6 Nov. 2019, **www.hmdb.org/m.asp?m=52988**

"Sand? Mine!" **www.climatechange.ie/sand-mine/**

"Slavery in the British and French Caribbean." *Wikipedia*, Wikimedia Foundation, 28 Oct. 2020, **en.wikipedia.org/wiki/Slavery_in_the_British_and_French_Caribbean**

Smil, Vaclav. *Making the Modern World: Materials and Dematerialization.* Wiley, 2013.

"Solons Act on Cement Plant Lease Deal." *Los Angeles Evening Herald*, 20 Apr. 1920, p. A9, **cdnc.ucr.edu/?a=d&d=LAH19200420.2.581&e=-------en--20--1--txt-txIN--------1**

Swanson, Ana. "How China Used More Cement in 3 Years than the U.S. Did in the Entire 20th Century." *The Washington Post*, 26 Apr. 2019, **www.washingtonpost.com/news/wonk/wp/2015/03/24/how-china-used-more-cement-in-3-years-than-the-u-s-did-in-the-entire-20th-century**

"The Triangular Trade." The Abolition Project, **abolition.e2bn.org/slavery_43.html**

4 Wheeling and Dealing

Autobiographical papers of Coy Burnett, date unknown

Wiggins, Susan. "Coy Burnett Field." *The Loop*, 20 Jan. 2018, **www.theloopnewspaper.com/story/2018/01/20/community/coy-burnett-field/4160.html**

5 Del Mar Before the Burnetts

"Chronology of the Indigenous Peoples of San Diego County." Compiled by Nancy Carol Carter, University of San Diego School of Law, University of San Diego, **www.sandiego.edu/native-american/chronology/**

Ewing, Nancy Hanks, and Alice Goodkind. *Del Mar: Looking Back.* Del Mar Historical Society, 1988.

"Old Del Mar." Del Mar Historical Society, **www.delmarhistoricalsociety.org/olde_del_mar.html**

Ray, Nancy. "Del Mar's Past Was Colorful, Checkered." *Los Angeles Times*, 25 Mar. 1985, **www.latimes.com/archives/la-xpm-1985-03-25-me-21357-story.html**

7 Houston

Ancestry.com / Birth and military records

8 *The First Architect*

Klinge, Jim. "Del Mar Castle." *Bubble Info*, 30 Mar. 2017, **www.bubbleinfo.com/2017/03/30/del-mar-castle/**

"Richard Requa." *Wikipedia,* Wikimedia Foundation, 16 Sept. 2020, **en.wikipedia.org/wiki/Richard_Requa**

Schibanoff, James M. "Requa & Jackson House in Peril." Save Our Heritage Organisation, 2004, **www.sohosandiego.org/reflections/2004-4/batchelder.htm**

9 *1929*

Ancestry.com/Census records

Ancestry.com/Shipping records

"Blue Riband." *Wikipedia*, Wikimedia Foundation, 8 Oct. 2020, **en.wikipedia.org/wiki/Blue_Riband**

Saez, Emmanuel, and Gabriel Zacman. "Wealth Inequality in the United States Since 1913: Evidence from Capitalized Income Tax Data." National Bureau of Economic Research, Oct. 2014.

10 *Hard Times*

"Great Depression History." **www.history.com/topics/great-depression/great-depression-history**

11 *Hoover Dam*

"Hoover Dam." *Wikipedia,* Wikimedia Foundation, 21 Nov. 2020, **en.m.wikipedia.org/wiki/Hoover_Dam**

Mead, Elwood and Ray Lyman Wilbur. "List of Principal Contracts." *The Construction of Hoover Dam: Preliminary Investigations, Design of Dam, and Progress of Construction.* United States Department of the Interior, 1933, p. 68.

13 *Santa Catalina*

Brooks, Cody. "The Hidden History of Catalina Island." *Peter Greenberg Travel Detective,* 24 Oct. 2018, **petergreenberg.com/2014/05/21/hidden-history-catalina-island/**

"Children, Leaders to Make Mass Joy-Junket to Island." The Bakersfield Californian , 13 July 1940, p. 7, **www.newspapers.com/clip/32343370/the-bakersfield-californian/**

"Chronology of the Indigenous Peoples of San Diego County." Compiled by Nancy Carol Carter, University of San Diego School of Law University of San Diego, **www.sandiego.edu/native-american/chronology/**

"History of Catalina Island." **www.visitcatalinaisland.com/island-info/history**

Johnson, Joan. "Mural Honors Vital Part of Tehachapi's History: Coy Burnett – The Man Behind The Name." Angelfire, *The Tehachapi News*, 23 June 2008, **www.angelfire.com/sd/thswarriors/news56.html**

"Kern Kiddies Take to Surf at Catalina." *The Bakersfield Californian*, 18 July 1938.

Marsa, Linda. "Reinterpreting an Ancient Island." *American Archaeology*, 2013, **www.csun.edu/sites/default/files/Catalina.pdf**

Monolith Portland Cement Company - Catalina Island 1939. **youtu.be/wXFDs_SXIVI**

Roberts, Rich. "Looking for Big Fish? Join the Club : At Catalina's Tuna Club, They're Hooked on Tradition." *Los Angeles Times*, 13 Oct. 1993, **www.latimes.com/archives/la-xpm-1993-10-13-sp-45385-story.html**

Tongva People, **tongvapeople.org/**

14 The Lookout

Brooks, Larry. Personal communication. 2019.

"Del Mar, California." *Wikipedia*, Wikimedia Foundation, 27 Oct. 2020, **en.wikipedia.org/wiki/Del_Mar,_California**

"Del Mar History." Visit Del Mar Village, 26 June 2019, **visitdelmarvillage.com/del-mar-history/**.

"Del Mar Fairgrounds: History: World War II Years: The Fairgrounds Joins the War Effort." **www.delmarfairgrounds.com/index.php?fuseaction=about.history_ww2**

Terwilliger, Don. Personal communication. 2016.

15 104 Fremont Place

Bengtson, John. "The Artist – Locations 1 of 5, Chaplin, and Pickford (Repost)." *Chaplin-Keaton-Lloyd Film Locations (and More)*, WordPress.com, 16 Feb. 2012, **silentlocations.wordpress.com/2012/02/16/the-artist-locations-chaplin-and-pickford-repost/**

Maginnis, Duncan. "Fremont Place." *Historic Los Angeles*, Blogger, 2016, **fremontplace.blogspot.com/2015/02/104-fremont-place-please-see-our.html**

Regan, Michael. *Mansions of Los Angeles*. Regan Publishing Company, 1965.

16 FIRE!

Burnett Gooding, Kingsbury. Personal communication. 2007.

"History." Rancho Santa Fe Fire Protection District, **www.rsf-fire.org/history**

19 Jessie

Ancestry.com / Birth, census, and shipping records

21 The Turf Club

"California Racing History." *Cal Racing*, **www.calracing.com/wp-content/uploads/2011/12/CMC_California-Racing-History.pdf**

"Del Mar Horse Racing History," 2020, **www.dmtc.com/season/history**

23 The Last Train to Clarksville

"America Meets the Beatles on 'The Ed Sullivan Show.'" History.com, A&E Television Networks, 16 Nov. 2009, **www.history.com/this-day-in-history/america-meets-the-beatles-on-the-ed-sullivan-show**

Gunderson, Chuck. "The Beatles Live! At Balboa Stadium 1965." *The Journal of San Diego History, Vol. 55*, pp. 21–36, **sandiegohistory.org/journal/v55-1/pdf/v55-1gunderson.pdf**

"The Helen Shapiro Tour, 1963." The Beatles – Tour Dates, **thebeatles.bizhat.com/tour_dates.htm**

Hurwitz, Matt. "The Beatles Made Music History at Shea Stadium." Variety, 15 Sept. 2016, **variety.com/2016/music/spotlight/beatles-music-history-shea-stadium-1201861551/**

"Last Train to Clarksville." *Wikipedia,* Wikimedia Foundation, 23 Oct. 2020, **en.wikipedia.org/wiki/Last_Train_to_Clarksville**

Leeds, Sarene. "11 Things You Might Not Know About *The Monkees.*" *Mental Floss,* 12 Sept. 2016, **mentalfloss.com/article/66101/11-things-you-might-not-know-about-monkees.**

"Live: Balboa Stadium, San Diego." *The Beatles Bible,* 27 Aug. 2018, **www.beatlesbible.com/1965/08/28/live-balboa-stadium-san-diego/**

"The Monkees." *TV Tropes,* **tvtropes.org/pmwiki/pmwiki.php/Music/TheMonkees**

"The Monkees." *Wikipedia,* Wikimedia Foundation, 21 Nov. 2020, **en.wikipedia.org/wiki/The_Monkees**

Sanford, Jay Allen. "RIP Davy Jones: the Monkees Once Turned Del Mar Into Clarksville." *San Diego Reader,* 29 Feb. 2012, **www.sandiegoreader.com/weblogs/jam-session/2012/feb/29/rip-davy-jones-the-monkees-once-turned-del-mar-int/**

Spizer, Bruce. "The Story Behind The Beatles on Ed Sullivan." *Internet Beatles Album,* **www.beatlesagain.com/the-beatles-on-ed-sullivan.html**

Varga, George. "The Beatles at Balboa Stadium: Yeah, Yeah, Yeah!" *San Diego Union-Tribune,* 8 Sept. 2016, **www.sandiegouniontribune.com/entertainment/music/sdut-beatles-at-balboa-stadium-fifty-year-anniversary-2015aug22-htmlstory.html**

24 Eventide

"Forest Lawn Glendale." *Cemetery Guide,* **www.cemeteryguide.com/ForestLawn-Glendale.jpg**

"Forest Lawn Memorial Park (Glendale)." *Wikipedia,* Wikimedia Foundation, 22 Nov. 2020, **en.m.wikipedia.org/wiki/Forest_Lawn_Memorial_Park_(Glendale).**

Wayne, Gary. "Forest Lawn Glendale, Part V." *Seeing Stars: Final Resting Places of the Stars,* **www.seeing-stars.com/Buried2/ForestLawnGlendale5.shtml**

25 Uncertain Times

Abbot, Chiquita. Personal communcation. 2016.

26 The Mysterious Mr. Smith

Dennis, Gregory. *Del Mar Surfcomber,* 1978.

27 Snakebit!

Dennis, Gregory. *Del Mar Surfcomber,* date unknown.

Ray, Nancy. "Hotel Proposal May Make It to Del Mar Ballot." *Los Angeles Times,* 2 Oct. 1985, **www.latimes.com/archives/la-xpm-1985-10-02-me-16080-story.html**

Ray, Nancy. "Resort at 'Snakewall' Proposed for Del Mar." *Los Angeles Times,* 6 Mar. 1985, **articles.latimes.com/1985-03-06/local/me-26298_1_del-mar**

Ray, Nancy. "Snakewall Owner Is Snakebit by Del Mar Politics." *Los Angeles Times,* 9 June 1991, **articles.latimes.com/1991-06-09/local/me-924_1_del-mar**

28 Rescued

Abbot, Chiquita. Personal communication. 2016.

"Home Depot Buys Catalog House: Home Depot..." *Chicago Tribune,* 27 Jan. 1997, **articles.chicagotribune.com/1997-01-27/news/9701280206_1_maintenance-warehouse-home-depot-maintenance-and-repair-supplies**

Neeley, Lucille, and Ron Neeley. Personal communication. 2015.

Neeley, Ron, and Lucille Neeley. Personal communication. 2016.

29 The Second Architect

Fracalossi, Igor. "Atalaya House / Alberto Kalach." ArchDaily, ArchDaily, 20 Sept. 2012, **www.archdaily.com/271981/atalaya-house-alberto-kalach**

Harlin, Claire. "Del Mar Historical Society Amping up Preservation Efforts." Del Mar Times, 14 Apr. 2013, **www.delmartimes.net/sddmt-del-mar-historical-society-amping-up-preservation-2013apr14-story.html**

"Meet the Architect Who Wants to Return Mexico City to Its Ancient Lakes." The Guardian, Guardian News and Media, 13 Nov. 2015, **www.theguardian.com/cities/2015/nov/13/alberto-kalach-return-mexico-city-ancient-lakes.**

Neeley, Lucille, and Ron Neeley. Personal interview. 2015.

Neeley, Lucille, and Ron Neeley. Personal interview. 2016.

TAX, Taller de Architectura X / Alberto Kallach, **www.kalach.com/**

Wiggins, Susan. "Coy Burnett Field." *The Loop,* 20 Jan. 2018, **www.theloopnewspaper.com/story/2018/01/20/community/coy-burnett-field/4160.html**

30 The Wall: Part Three

Moriel Trejo, Hortensia. Personal communication. 2016. C

Index

C

D

E

F

G

H

I, J

K

L

M

About the Author

Brier Miller Minor grew up in Southern California, where she got to spend memorable Augusts at her grandparents' estate in Del Mar, enjoying the beach and the seemingly endless days of summer. She left California for Colorado College in 1968 and moved to the Midwest in 1976. After a brief career as an elementary school teacher, she found herself drawn to counseling. She earned a master's degree in Marriage and Family Therapy at the University of Wisconsin–Stout and has passionately practiced and taught family therapy for close to 40 years. In 2014 she received the Distinguished Service Award from the Minnesota Association for Marriage and Family Therapy.

Brier lives in Minneapolis, where she and her partner, Bruce, are lucky enough to have all three of their kids and eight grandchildren close by. Already established as a productive author in her profession, she began writing creatively in the early 2000s and has been part of a writing group for more than 10 years. She has never forgotten her idyllic summers walking the wall in Del Mar, with its challenges and unexpected revelations; the opportunity to write a book about it is the fulfillment of a long-held dream.

"It's been a rewarding journey of remembering and of discovery," she says, "about a significant time in Southern California history and about my own family, and a source of insight into how deeply our early life shapes our patterns of communication and attachment."